The Other Windrush

The Other Windrush

Legacies of Indenture in Britain's Caribbean Empire

Edited by
Maria del Pilar Kaladeen
and David Dabydeen

PLUTO PRESS

First published 2021 by Pluto Press
345 Archway Road, London N6 5AA

www.plutobooks.com

The editors are grateful to the Ameena Gafoor Institute for the Study of Indentureship and Its Legacies for supporting the publication of this book.

British Library Cataloguing in Publication Data
A catalogue record for this book is available from the British Library

ISBN   978 0 7453 4355 6   Hardback
ISBN   978 0 7453 4354 9   Paperback
ISBN   978 0 7453 4358 7   PDF
ISBN   978 0 7453 4356 3   EPUB
ISBN   978 0 7453 4357 0   Kindle

This book is printed on paper suitable for recycling and made from fully managed and sustained forest sources. Logging, pulping and manufacturing processes are expected to conform to the environmental standards of the country of origin.

Typeset by Stanford DTP Services, Northampton, England

Simultaneously printed in the United Kingdom and United States of America

Contents

List of figures

Dedicated to the memory of Krishna Prasad (born 1932,
British Guiana; died 2019, London)

And with love to Surujpaul Kaladeen, dreamer and Windrusher
(born 1938, British Guiana)

Introduction: 'My Father's Journey Made Me Who I Am'

Maria del Pilar Kaladeen and David Dabydeen

Despite the strong sense of Caribbean identity that connects the contributors to this book, many of us have experienced, throughout our lives, the blank looks of those who have struggled to place us when we respond to that most loaded of questions, 'Where are you from?' Far too few people in the United Kingdom know about the system of indenture in the Caribbean and the people of Chinese and Indian descent that it left in the region. Fewer still are aware that alongside African-Caribbean people, the descendants of these indentured labourers formed part of the Windrush generation of migrants from the region to Britain during 1948–1971.[1] While this book reflects on the challenges experienced by a community who have effectively lived their lives as a minority within a minority, it is also a celebration of what has been made possible in spite of our invisibility to the general population and through the creative ways we have resisted the silence that surrounds our cultural history.

---

1 It is important to note that ships carrying Caribbean migrants arrived before this date. However, the 1948 Commonwealth Act, which reaffirmed the right to British nationality of citizens of the Commonwealth, was an attempt to foster an environment that would enable men and women from across the British Empire to live and work in the UK, fulfilling the nation's urgent need for labour and helping to rebuild cities devastated by the Second World War. The establishment of the National Health Service in the same year created a significant part of the need for a workforce who largely came from the Caribbean, India and Pakistan. Contributions in this book show how people from the Caribbean responded to this call for labour; coming to train as nurses, work in the army or study for a number of other professions.

From 1838 to 1917, the populations of British Caribbean colonies were transformed by a system of unfree labour called indenture. This system brought Indian and Chinese people to labour on plantations that produced mainly sugar, but also cocoa, coconut and rubber. Although they came to these colonies on temporary contracts, the majority of these workers never returned home, and despite their numbers, their migration story is largely unknown in Britain, the country that directed the fate of these men, women and children. It is unsurprising that Indian-Caribbean and Chinese-Caribbean people should continue to be largely absent from European versions of colonial history. What has always superseded the discussion of Britain's benefit from close to two centuries of African slavery in the Caribbean is the narrative of imperial benevolence that continually draws attention to the British abolition of the slave trade. Traditionally, this narrative has ignored the system of indentured labour that supplanted it.

It is indicative of the entirely venal nature of Caribbean plantation society that alternative sources of labour were sought even before the end of slavery and the apprenticeship system in the Caribbean. Discussions about the possibility of taking Chinese labourers to the British Caribbean took place as early as 1810. Portuguese indentured labourers from Madeira preceded the Indian presence in Guyana (British Guiana), and other groups of European labourers, as well as indentured Africans, were later employed as a replacement workforce. Although the first Indian indentured labourers were brought to Guyana in 1838, they were shortly followed by arrivals to Trinidad in 1845 and later arrivals in smaller numbers to Grenada, Jamaica, St Kitts and Nevis, St Lucia, St Vincent and Belize (British Honduras). By far the largest number of labourers went to Guyana and Trinidad. Chinese indentured labourers arrived in Guyana and Trinidad in 1853 and Jamaica in 1854. By the time the indenture system had been abolished in 1917, close to 18,000 Chinese and almost 450,000 Indians had been brought to the British Caribbean.

Indenture in the Caribbean was defined by a clear pattern of abuses against labourers, followed by reforms of the system that were intended to prevent their further exploitation and maltreatment. These rarely addressed the worst abuses of indenture which could see potential recruits deceived about the type of work they would do and the length of the voyage they would embark on. Shipped across the Atlantic to work on plantations for periods of three or five years, labourers were encouraged to re-indenture for a further term, sometimes with the promise of land in lieu of a return passage. The indentured frequently occupied the same meagre shacks which had housed the enslaved Africans before them. Strict labour laws bound workers to the plantations, and governmental inquiries brought to light repeated cases of plantation managers and overseers abusing their authority by physically attacking and sexually exploiting the workers. The workers' resistance to what can only be described in many cases as a semi-penal existence can be traced in records that show their ability to organise against oppressive plantation managers. This resistance meant that the system frequently teetered insecurely rather than confidently, and was punctuated by strikes and uprisings.

Within decades of the inception of indenture, a minority of Chinese-Caribbean and Indian-Caribbean people were able to access schools and liberate their children from the plantation system. In a few cases they were able to go overseas for tertiary education. Accordingly, even before Indian-Caribbean migrants left the region as part of the Windrush generation, an Indian-Guyanese man named William Hewley Wharton had completed his study of medicine at the University of Edinburgh in 1899 and returned to the colony to work as a doctor. The Chinese-Trinidadian bacteriologist Joseph Lennox Pawan, whose work on rabies had global significance, also studied at Edinburgh University, completing his degree in 1912. Achievements like this are likely to have been a source of inspiration to others, who saw in Britain a place where they might access higher education and wider opportunities. There is no doubt that these ideas filtered down to many in the Windrush generation, and this idea was explored in a recent article by the academic Heidi Safia Mirza, the daughter of an Indian-Trinidadian who arrived in England in 1951 aboard the *Columbe*.[2]

Despite the fact that they have emerged from a little-known community, descendants of indenture have participated in the formation of a British Caribbean identity from the earliest moments of their arrival. It is widely recognised that the National Health Service (NHS) is indebted to the workers of the Windrush generation, and a number of contributors to this book (Mr Gee, Maria del Pilar Kaladeen, Nalini Mohabir, Jonathan Phang and Bob Ramdhanie) had parents or relatives who worked in the NHS. Indian-Trinidadian novelists Samuel Selvon and V.S. Naipaul, who both arrived in the UK in the 1950s, ignited literary fires that inspired later Windrush writers like David Dabydeen, whose poetry volume *Coolie Odyssey* (Watton-at-Stone, UK: Hansib Publications, 1988) is a journey into the double migrations of Indian indenture and Windrush. Dabydeen's work as an academic and writer was made possible not only by the creation of the Centre for Caribbean Studies at the University of Warwick in 1984, but also through the establishment of publishing houses which supported the work of Caribbean writers and scholars.

Jeremy Poynting's Leeds-based Peepal Tree Press, for example, published work by the Chinese-Guyanese writers Jan Lowe Shinebourne and Meiling Jin. Jin's poetic work *Gifts from my Grandmother* (London: Sheba Feminist Press, 1985), deserves a special mention here, not merely for the spare, precise and powerful poetry, but also for its important recounting of Jin's early experiences of life in the UK as a Windrush child of Chinese ancestry. Peepal Tree's contribution to Indian-Caribbean litera-

---

2 '"The Golden Fleece": The *Windrush* Quest for Educational Desire', www.bl.uk/windrush/articles/the-golden-fleece-the-windrush-quest-for-educational-desire, accessed 6 January 2020.

ture through the publication of authors, both in Britain and in the Caribbean, is unparalleled. Indian-Guyanese Windrusher Arif Ali, who founded Hansib Publications in 1970, played an important role in the academic development of Indian-Caribbean studies (led by David Dabydeen and Clem Seecharan[3]) in the UK. In 1987, Hansib published the ground-breaking *India in the Caribbean* and *Benevolent Neutrality: Indian Government Policy and Labour Migration to British Guiana, 1854–1884* and republished one of the founding texts of indentureship studies, Hugh Tinker's *A New System of Slavery: The Export of Indian Labour Overseas 1830–1920*.[4] The first two of these books were timed to commemorate 150 years since the arrival of the first indentured labourers in Guyana in 1838, and alongside publications in the University of Warwick-Macmillan Caribbean series, became key texts for the next generation of indenture scholars.[5]

Beyond educational institutions, Roy Sawh and barrister Rudy Narayan — whose life journalist Lainy Malkani reflects upon in this anthology — focused on work that can be interpreted as expressions of solidarity with African-Caribbean communities who bore the brunt of the institutional discrimination that marked life in the UK in the 1970s and 1980s – Sawh through his public speaking at Hyde Park during 1958–1989, and Narayan through his legal work from his offices in Brixton. Their efforts defied the divisive politics that marked Guyana following the race riots of the 1960s (see Elly Niland's Chapter 3 in this volume) and which feature heavily as the inspiration behind the work of spoken word poet Mr Gee in Chapter 10. Bob Ramdhanie's oral history interview in Chapter 5 goes some way to showing a con-

---

3   Professor Clem Seecharan was Head of the Centre for Caribbean Studies at London Metropolitan University between 1993 and 2012.
4   Originally published by Oxford University Press in 1974.
5   This work has culminated in the establishment in 2020 of the Ameena Gafoor Institute for the Study of Indentureship and Its Legacies. Based in the UK, it is the first centre of its kind.

temporary audience what Tao Leigh Goffe refers to in Chapter 8 as the 'strategic essentialism of Black as a political identity' at this time. As Mr Gee's chapter shows, however, these early solidarities became harder to locate in the decades that followed, and he reflects on this in his recounting of life in the 1990s as the child of an African-Ugandan father and an Indian-Guyanese mother.

In 2018, the 70th anniversary of the arrival of the *Empire Windrush* at Tilbury Docks was marred by revelations that elderly and vulnerable members of the Windrush generation and their children were wrongly threatened with deportation, and in some cases incorrectly removed from the UK. The justifiable public outrage over these events surprised the current government, whose creation of an annual Windrush Day (21 June) was interpreted by many as a hasty scramble to repair the severely damaged public relations that resulted from these tragic events. Both the anniversary and the scandal have prompted a movement towards a wider understanding of the Windrush generation and its lesser-known histories. The Migration Museum's 2017–2018 exhibition *No Turning Back: Seven Migration Moments That Changed Britain* displayed the family history of one storyteller who was both a descendant of Indian indentured labourers and the child of a Windrush migrant. The British Library's online exhibition *Windrush Stories* includes accounts of the experiences of descendants of indenture, and Charlie Brinkhurst Cuff's *Mother Country: Real Stories of the Windrush Children* (London: Headline, 2018) contains tales by Windrush children of Chinese, Indian and Jewish descent.

While this anthology focuses on the mobilities and migrations triggered by the creation of the system of indenture in the case of Guyana, indigenous people of Amerindian heritage also migrated to the UK as part of the Windrush generation. Notable examples include the writer Pauline Melville (winner of the *Guardian* Fiction Prize and the Commonwealth Writers' Prize) and the artist George Simon (winner of the Anthony N. Sabga Award for Excellence).[6]

Speaking about the first generation of Indian indentured labourers to the Caribbean, historian Clem Seecharan has used the term 'collective amnesia' to describe the community's silent agreement to forget the complex reasons that motivated each individual departure from India. The work of historians focusing on these varied 'push factors' tells us that these could include severe poverty, famine, domestic violence, a need to hide from authorities or being coerced by recruiters. Jan Lowe Shinebourne's excellent novel *The Last Ship* (Leeds, UK: Peepal Tree Press, 2015) is an exploration of the roots and consequences of similar modes of forgetting in a Chinese-Guyanese family. As far as the children of the 'Other Windrush' are concerned, these first-generation silences could sometimes be fortified by their own parents' reticence to discuss their early lives in the UK in order to shield their children from painful stories of discrimination. While understanding their origins, this book seeks to challenge these silences, sharing aspects of the stories of our parents, grandparents and great-grandparents, and showing how much our own lives have been defined by the bravery that motivated their multiple journeys, and their lives.

The seeds of this anthology were sown in 2017, when the editors convened an oral history panel at the University of London to amplify the voices of descendants of indenture who were also part of the Windrush generation. Sharing aspects of her father's voyage across the Atlantic with the audience, Heidi Safia Mirza reflected on what this meant for her. 'My father's journey', said Mirza, 'made me who I am.' One cannot look upon Mirza's work as an academic who has sought to expose the injustices encountered at the intersections of race and gender and not immediately

6   In her essay 'Wearing Where You're at: Immigration and UK Fashion' in *The Good Immigrant* (London: Unbound, 2016, pp. 144–58), writer Sabrina Mahfouz shares the story of her Guyanese grandfather, of Amerindian and Madeiran heritage, who came to the UK in the 1950s.

understand that her comment encapsulates the understanding that at its best, to be part of the Windrush generation was to belong to a community of resisters whose support for one another operated in defiance of the hostile environment recounted here.

1

What's in a Face?

Jonathan Phang

I found growing up in London during the 1970s very confusing. Wherever I went, I never seemed to fit in; to me, my facial features looked weird, and as a result, I felt like I had nothing in common with anyone. Unsurprisingly, I became introverted, and often felt like a square peg trying to squeeze into a round hole. During puberty, people were either intrigued by my indefinable looks or threatened by them. Due to my height, large frame and wavy hair, people presumed that my heritage was Samoan or Tongan, and expected me to be good at rugby. Sadly, I wasn't, and I became the class booby prize on the playing field, as well as off it.

Although my home life was privileged and loving, I felt displaced there, as I did at school. My family expressed themselves in a completely different way to everyone else. We were boisterous, ate Caribbean food, and listened to reggae and calypso instead of rock and pop. My father looked Chinese, but sounded West Indian (unless he was engaging with an English person, at which point he'd affect an accent that was more English than the English). I yearned to blend in and feel normal; instead, I felt awkward, isolated and embarrassed about who I was, but despite this, I never felt ashamed of my parents.

I was aware that my weekends were different from those of my classmates, so on Monday, I would play down what I had done. Most people went to the pictures on Saturday morning, followed by football with their dad, or perhaps a sleepover with friends. On Sunday, they might have a roast dinner with their grandparents, followed by a country walk, board games, telly or something else that they might enjoy. In other words, life centred around *them*. In contrast, we spent our weekends indulging my father. Generally, this meant entertaining several of his friends, who would spend Saturday afternoons in front of the television, studying form and gambling on the horses, while eating us out of house and home. Meanwhile, my mother and the female visitors would spend all day cooking and serving the men. I sought refuge in the kitchen and gratefully learned how to cook curry and roti, pepperpot, garlic pork, chow mein, pine tarts and patties, along with various other Guyanese and Chinese delicacies. For hours on end, I listened with great interest to their gossip and sentimental anecdotes from 'home', and I wondered, had their journey to the motherland met their expectations, or did they still dream of more?

Our Sundays were usually spent in Chinatown, wearing our best clothes and devouring our body weight in dim sum. We would then get bored listening to my father holding court with half of the West Indian Social Club and other Chinese Caribbean immigrants, who spent their day off liming (doing nothing in particular) in Gerrard Street. I kept out of my father's way. My mother instilled in us that children should be seen and not heard, and that as Lord master and provider, our father needed rest and should be allowed to enjoy his day off with his friends without interruption.

In my mind's eye, the 'home' that everyone kept going on about was a tropical paradise, bursting with grand palm-lined boulevards, flanked by elegant whitewashed wooden houses, embellished with filigree fretwork, shaded by Demerara shutters and flaming flamboyant trees. This utopic world of my naive imagination knew nothing of what it meant to be born in a country colonised by Europeans, where Africans had been enslaved and where Portuguese, Chinese and Indians had been indentured labourers. No one, including my family and teachers, could shed any light on the history of my cultural heritage, Guyana, or any other of Britain's' colonies for that matter. I had no perception of what being British was supposed to mean to someone like me, and I certainly couldn't understand why my family held Queen and Country in such high regard. To this day, few people know about the British Empire's system of indentured servitude that resulted in Guyana's Indian, Chinese and Portuguese population and which is part of my own family history.

My parents' love story was legendary in Georgetown and is fondly remembered by those involved with their courtship. They had met by chance, one afternoon in 1950, while my mother was walking home from St Rose's convent school with her classmates. From all accounts, it was love at first sight; my mother was what

Figure 1.1 My mother Maureen. (Photo courtesy of Jonathan Phang)

would have then been termed a 'mulatto', and few could pinpoint where her 'exotic' looks originated (see Figure 1.1). She could have been from anywhere between Latin America and the Middle East. She had razor-sharp cheekbones, dark, deep-set, almond-shaped eyes with perfectly arched eyebrows, and an engaging dimple on her left cheek. She was statuesque and beautiful; this gave her an air of confidence beyond her years.

It took a whole year before the love-struck pair went out on their first date. My mother was only 15 when they met; my father was eight years her senior. My father was mindful and wary of their age difference; he told her that he would not court her until she had graduated from high school. Despite her frustration, my mother was confident that he was the man for her. She proudly told all her school friends that she would marry Roy Phang and have plenty of chubby Chinese babies. She waited patiently for the year to pass. In the mean time, she befriended Roy's cousin Margery and engaged more with the Chinese community, ensuring that he was aware of her every move, and making it impossible for him to get her out of his mind. My honourable father remained true to his word and stayed away from her until she completed her education. Occasionally, he'd send her affectionate tokens via cousin Margery to keep her interested. He sensed that their relationship was never going to be easy as he knew there was the matter of race, and Maureen's tyrannical father, Cyril (see Figure 1.2).

The Chinese community was one of the smallest minority communities in Guyana, and they tended to keep themselves to themselves; they rarely married 'out', especially to a 'creole'.

My grandfather, Cyril, was the eldest of seven children born to John and Mary Elma. John was the favourite illegitimate child of a Dutch Jewish plantation owner named Bollers. Bollers was originally from Paramaribo and had several Amerindian and 'mulatto' mistresses. He was unlikely to have been aware of the number of children that he had fathered. However, as John's mother was one of his preferred paramours, he chose to recognise him, and though

Figure 1.2 Cyril Bollers, my maternal grandfather. (Photo courtesy of Jonathan Phang)

he eventually grew tired of John's mother, he spotted something
special in the handsome, young John and removed him from the
cane fields (and his mother) to have him privately educated. John
was a charismatic and naturally intelligent child who thrived at
school and took exams in his stride. He graduated from Edinburgh
University in the 1890s and returned to the West Indies with a
First Class Honours degree and a white Scottish bride, whose
looks were at best considered 'handsome'. At that time, Georgetown, with its pretty tree-lined streets and picturesque canals, was
known as the Garden City of the Caribbean, and Guyana itself
was one of the most lucrative jewels in Britain's colonial crown,
with fertile plains, mineral mines and dense rain forests. John's rise

to wealth and power was rapid. Among other things, he became Chairman of the country's largest drugstore, Secretary of the British Guiana & Trinidad Mutual Fire Insurance Company and a member of the Georgetown Town Council.

Mary Elma enjoyed the trappings that came with being an affluent white mistress in nineteenth-century Georgetown society. She grabbed every advantage without conscience or empathy and ruled her household with an iron fist. She was the driving force behind her husband's success, and for a time they were Georgetown's glittering couple, but as John's star rose, his interest in his wife waned. She had convinced herself that bearing children would solve their problems. John did not know the exact details of his heritage, so he concocted a convincing tale that satisfied even the most curious minds, including that of Mary Elma. However, when her first child was born (my grandfather Cyril), it was evident from the baby's physical appearance that there was far more to John's story than he had revealed, and she began to question his motives for marrying her.

Her misgivings were in vain; she had made her bed, and she had no choice other than to lie in it. Cyril's birth ignited a vicious streak in Mary Elma's character, and there were times when she could barely stand to look at him. As her other six children were born, each fairer than the last, her scorn for Cyril grew. He was not allowed to play with his siblings in public, and while the family entertained, his mother often hid Cyril in the attic, refusing to mention him. Cyril became withdrawn and developed a nervous disposition. Mary Elma's decision to send him away to school in England as soon as he was old enough exacerbated his idiosyncrasies and affected his mental and physical well-being for the rest of his life.

Cyril returned to Georgetown at the turn of the twentieth century, broken by the brutality of British public school. He was the only pupil of colour, and he suffered daily bullying and humiliation from students and teachers alike. Cyril was naturally bright and had aspirations to become a doctor; however, he contracted osteomyelitis at school and endured several operations that interrupted his studies. With his ambitions thwarted, Cyril felt that his only hope of being accepted into society and pleasing his parents would be to marry a white girl and start a family.

My grandmother Maude was a beautiful 'local white' from Barbados (see Figure 1.3). She was descended from indentured servants and labourers from Scotland and Madeira, who most likely met and worked on the same plantation. After emancipation, formerly enslaved Blacks could train in all key trades, so there was no longer a need for cheap white labour. The local whites were unwilling to work alongside the freed Blacks (who were less expensive to hire). Instead, they chose to emigrate to other British colonies to find better opportunities.

Figure 1.3 My maternal grandmother Maude.
Her eldest son, John, is pictured standing.
(Photo courtesy of Jonathan Phang)

By the time Maude arrived in Georgetown, she had blossomed into a sultry-looking young woman. She had waist-length auburn hair, a curvy figure and sparkling hazel-coloured eyes. Her pale complexion had deliberately been kept out of the sun and belied her Portuguese heritage. Maude's people were thrilled for their daughter to be marrying into such a distinguished family, but Mary Elma was incandescent with rage, and she was, as always, less than impressed with Cyril. She considered Maude to be a 'redleg', which in her opinion was the lowest of the low, and made it clear that Maude would never be welcome into her family.

'She is a good woman, and she has such a beautiful face!' Cyril protested.

'But it's what's in her face that matters. With that "Putagee" widow's peak and red skin, her face says it all! She's not even good enough to be one of my maids! Never bring that shameful low-class white into my house. Ever!'

Cyril and Maude's wedding was a sombre event that my maternal great-grandparents did not attend, and Maude was never welcomed into her in-laws' home. It appeared that there was nothing Cyril could do to earn approval from his parents. His father had pretty much written him off, but he did pull strings and find him a job as a floor manager at G. Bettencourt & Co., a lowly position for someone from such a distinguished and ambitious family, but respectable nonetheless.

I believe that Cyril truly loved Maude. As a child, he told me many times the story of how he fell in love with her beautiful face at first sight, and how her waist-length wavy hair made her look like an angel. By the time Maude was pregnant, within a year of getting married, her life was no better than that of one of Mary Elma's maids. Cyril had inherited his mother's vicious streak, and unleashed all of his frustrations on Maude. With each year, Cyril grew more angry and bitter. His eldest son John physically resembled him the most, but unlike Cyril, he was a spirited and strong-willed boy who hated how Cyril treated his mother and younger siblings, and he wasn't afraid to let him know it. Cyril was brutal when crossed by John, and subjected him to regular beatings. Maude couldn't bear to witness such violence, and she feared for her son's life. As a result, John was sent to live with his spinster aunts, and never returned home. It took a decade and a change of country before John got to know my mother again. Maude continued to live her life under duress, and inevitably, it wasn't long before another of her children experienced Cyril's wrath. Despite his misdemeanours, Maude remained empathetic and loyal to Cyril. She compensated for his abusive behaviour as best she could by being a devoted mother and spoiling her beloved offspring with an understanding ear and a broad repertoire of delicious homecooked food. In contrast, my father's upbringing was comparatively idyllic, although his background was similarly lurid and convoluted.

It was in 1853, when the British turned to China for the additional recruitment of indentured labourers, that the first batch of Chinese male 'cane reapers' landed in Georgetown. Among them was my great-great-grandfather Li. Li was a Hakka Chinese fleeing from the T'ai P'ing Rebellion. In an attempt to hide his true identity from the authorities and avoid conviction, he cut off his pigtail, made his way to Canton, offered himself for indentured labour, and boarded a boat bound for British Guiana.

During the arduous three-month voyage, Li developed a close friendship with a man of Indian descent from the Middle Kingdom. They shared a similar background, and both came from societies which regarded women as inferior and only necessary for household management and procreation. Both men believed in the importance of continuing the family line. Chinese women were not allowed into British Guiana until several years after the men arrived, so in an act of friendship, his friend loaned his wife to Li, to carry on his family name. I can only imagine what this meant for the woman who would carry this baby. In all likelihood, she would have had no choice regarding the conception of this child.

My great-grandfather William Lee (see Figure 1.4) was born at their plantation, on the West bank of the Demerara, and was brought up solely by Li. William's earliest recollection was of being carried on his father's back and left on the banks of the cane fields, one end of a string tied around his waist and the other tied to his father's. At the end of his indentureship, instead of returning to China, Li used what little money he had saved and took William to Georgetown, where he attended the Charlestown School. William thrived at school, and after graduating, he became the first Chinese man to be appointed Manager of the Wholesale Provision Department of Booker Brothers Ltd. The Bookers empire was so powerful that locals often referred

Figure 1.4 William Adrian Lee, my paternal great-grandfather. (Photo courtesy of Jonathan Phang)

to the colony as 'Bookers Guiana'. William married Piat Poon
(known as Eva), who, like him, was born in Guyana to indentured
parents. They were first-generation Chinese-Indian Guyanese,
who wanted to remain British citizens and contribute to society.
They became devout Christians and believed in traditional family
values; they bore ten children, nine of whom lived into adulthood.
Neither of them lived long lives, but their time on earth was happy
and fruitful.

Their eldest daughter Amy (see Figure 1.5) was a naturally
kind-hearted and thoughtful child; she enjoyed looking after her
younger siblings, and loved experimenting in the kitchen. By the
time Amy met my grandfather, Joseph Phang, she was adept in
all aspects of housekeeping and was a renowned cook. Joseph
was a placid, small-framed man who had good prospects as a
surveyor, but needed that little extra nudge to help him realise
his potential. Amy Lee was just the ticket. Amy was no shrinking
violet; she was ambitious, resourceful, entrepreneurial and fiercely
protective of her family. She wholeheartedly ruled the roost, and
worked tirelessly to ensure that her children were all educated and
equipped for the world. To make extra money, Amy made picnic
baskets containing her original recipes. After reading an article in
Vogue, she travelled to New York to learn how to perm hair. While
away, Amy wrote to her children every day to share details of her
adventures and remind them of their responsibilities. She brought
back the first Joyner permanent wave machine to Georgetown,
and given the fact that the local population was mostly Indian and
Chinese, naturally she made a killing.

Amy died unexpectedly within days of my father's 25th birthday.
She was yet to turn 50. I don't believe that he ever recovered from
her loss. During his final days, he spoke with clarity of no one else
but his beloved mother, Amy. *The Daily Chronicle* commented:

With the passing of Amy Phang, another kind lady has checked
out. She was a fitting example of a wife, mother and friend.

Figure 1.5   Amy Phang, my paternal
grandmother. (Photo courtesy of
Jonathan Phang)

One of those remarkable persons in our community to whom
someday this country will erect a monument with the simple
inscription: TO THE GREATEST WOMEN IN GUIANA.

Of all the ancestors I never had the opportunity to meet, Amy is
the one who intrigues me the most. Everyone adored her, and I
wish that I had known her.

My father, Roy, was a popular boy with a winning smile and an
infectious laugh. He excelled on the sports field and won many
accolades for his tennis skills; he was also a crucial player in the

Queen's College football team. His mother had insisted that he learn how to play the piano, and eventually he could play any tune by ear, and loved entertaining people. Before he met my mother, he had several girlfriends, and was even once engaged to a Trinidadian named June Chan. However, after that chance meeting on the seawall, he, like my mother, was smitten and broke off his engagement. He told all of his friends that when the time was right, he would spend the rest of his life with Maureen Bollers.

Cyril had grand plans for his daughter, which did not include her cavorting with a 'Chiney coolie-boy'. Cyril's disdain for their relationship was relentless, and he stopped at nothing to try and prevent them from seeing one another, from breaking sticks on her back to cutting up her dresses into thousands of pieces. However, love prevailed, and with the help of their family and friends, the love struck pair found ways of meeting. Cyril's destructive behaviour continued for the next two years until one morning, in January 1953, just after my mother's 18th birthday, he invited her for a drive, took her to the docks, and put her on a steamship to England. He had secretly packed her bags and hid them in the boot of his car. Little did he realise my mother was thrilled; she was happy to be getting away from him, and she did not doubt that my father would follow her. However, her feelings of joy did not last for long, as she never got her sea legs and worried about her mother desperately. The passage took several weeks from Georgetown to Plymouth via Paramaribo and Madeira. Luckily for my mother, one of Roy's favourite cousins, Joan Whitehead, was in the cabin opposite hers. Her roommate, Elsa Mansell, was a lovely person too, so my mother was well looked after during the voyage and made friends for life.

Upon arrival in Plymouth, and to her great surprise, my mother was met from the ship by her estranged brother John, who had recently completed his National Service in the UK and had joined the British Army. John had organised digs for his sister in a female-only boarding house off the Fulham Palace Road. The landlady, Doris, was a maternal, buxom 'salt of the earth' East End widow who had spent time in Guyana and had fallen in love with its people. So, in an era when boarding house windows displayed signs reading 'No Blacks, No Dogs, No Irish', Doris exclusively welcomed people from the Caribbean. Doris knew of my parents' predicament from Uncle John, so letters from Georgetown were already waiting to greet my mother. Cyril had packed one of his old overcoats into mum's suitcase, which otherwise contained an array of brightly coloured cotton summer dresses. Within 24 hours of arriving on British shores, my mother caught the worst cold of her life.

As predicted, my father followed my mother to London in 1954. During their courtship, he lived in Barnes, in a room rented from another war widow named Nipsey. Both landladies supported my parents' relationship and regularly invited the other for Sunday lunch, but strict rules applied, and they were never left alone. My mother found a local clerical job, and my father worked nights in a Lyons cake factory supervising the Swiss rolls while he studied dentistry at Guy's Hospital during the day.

Their only opportunity to be alone was on Saturday afternoons, when they would go to the cinema and watch the same film over and over again. It gave them a chance to have a cuddle and to keep warm, because it was cheaper than feeding the gas meter at home. My parents did not get married (see Figure 1.6) until my father had qualified as a dental surgeon in 1959. The Commonwealth countries were crying out for skilled professionals in those days. Several of my father's peers took advantage of the appealing tax breaks and non-domiciled status offered to doctors and dentists willing to move abroad. However, my father felt grateful to Britain for the life that he was able to create for himself, and he remained loyal to the National Health Service for his entire career.

By the time I came along in 1966, my parents had 'made it'; it had taken them 15 years and a lot of hard work, but now my mother only had to work part-time, and they lived in a respectable

Figure 1.6   My parents on their wedding day (Photo courtesy of Jonathan Phang)

tree-lined suburban street with their three healthy children. Like many immigrants and people of colour, they felt that they had to work harder and be better than their neighbours. Outwardly, they adopted the customs of their chosen country and tried their best to blend in, but behind closed doors, their domain remained Guyanese to the core.

The 1950s and 1960s were a period of political unrest in Guyana. Both the British colonial government and the US Central Intelligence Agency interfered heavily in the country's path to independence, fostering ethnic divides that resulted in turbulent riots and bloodshed. Guyana eventually achieved independence from the United Kingdom in 1966, and declared itself a 'cooperative republic' on 23 February 1970. Forbes Burnham succeeded in becoming Guyana's first prime minister; he immediately nationalised the foreign companies that dominated the sugar and bauxite industries, and vowed to guide the country into a new socialist era. Adopting an autarky policy, Burnham banned all forms of imports into the country, including flour and rice.

Life in the once genteel, affluent 'Garden City of the Caribbean, became dangerous, corrupt and entrenched in economic poverty. On a practical level, food and toiletries became scarce, taxes were prohibitive, and power outages, along with water shortages, were all too regular.

In 1970, my maternal grandparents, Cyril and Maude, boarded a plane and arrived in London with a suitcase each and currency worth nothing. My parents had organised rooms for them in Acton through friends of friends, and found Cyril a job as a caretaker at a local primary school. Within a year, my paternal grandfather Joseph and his second wife Phyllis escaped George-town and came to live with us in our house.

Our family life changed irrevocably. My mother was run ragged between doing the school run, the housework and travelling back and forth to Acton to help Maude, who was too old and scared to find her own way in a new country. Cyril was as miserable as ever; he was ridiculed and subjected to daily racial abuse at work. At home, he continued to take his frustrations out on poor Maude.

My step-grandmother Phyllis was not a jolly lady; in fact, her countenance and demeanour rivalled Cyril's. To me, Phyllis looked ancient. She was a small, frail-looking second-generation Portu-guese Guyanese widow who had not been blessed with children from her first marriage to Mr De Souza and was overwhelmed by having to now live with three of her new husband's grandchildren. My mother found sharing a kitchen with her intolerable, and the atmosphere between them was palpable. To keep the peace, Phyllis spent most of her time in her room and survived on a diet of sardines and peanut butter.

Phyllis was an accomplished landscape painter and adept at sewing crochet doilies. During the years that she lived with us, she worked as a part-time seamstress at Marshall & Snelgrove in

Oxford Street. I am ashamed to admit that this is all I know about her. I feel sure that I would have found her a lot more enjoyable had I been older. My father worked every hour that God sent just to keep the wolf from the door, and the poor man was permanently exhausted. My siblings and I had to be fed and watered before he returned home from work so that he could have a moment of peace to himself.

Life remained challenging and complicated for all of us. By 1973, we had lost Maude and Joseph. Phyllis went her separate way, and Cyril came to live with us until he died in 1983. My parents told us nothing about Cyril's antics until after he died, for fear of influencing us against him. Their experience of migration had given them kind and generous hearts. Still, I often wonder if they ever felt genuinely settled in this country. I feel sure that they had many moments of joy, but as my siblings and I grew, the cultural differences became more apparent, and my parents spent many years being at odds with this country. I will always remember my parents as the ultimate hosts, who continually left their friends wanting more. Their lives were short, both died in their sixties, and I miss them every minute of every day. Like most orphans, I find myself wishing that I had known more, said more and done more.

2

Black Turkey

David Dabydeen

In 1985, the newly established Centre for Caribbean Studies at the University of Warwick, under the visionary Directorship of Professor Alistair Hennessy, embarked on a short-lived oral history project – short-lived because the Centre had the tiniest of budgets. The Centre was an umbrella organisation consisting of academics from the English, History, Sociology, Education and Comparative American Studies Departments who generously volunteered their services and part-time involvement in the academic programme of the Centre. Following the 1980–1981 'race riots' in London, Bristol and elsewhere, and the American invasion of Grenada in 1983, Professor Hennessy had persuaded the University to set up the very first Centre for Caribbean Studies at a British university. The University succumbed to his charisma and power of argument. The Caribbean had been among Britain's most valuable possessions for two centuries, the revenues from slavery and slave-produced commodities greatly enriching the country, and as Eric Williams argued, helped to fund the Industrial Revolution, never mind financial institutions (banking, insurance). By the 1980s, all was forgotten. So the Centre was given a few hundred pounds to conduct its business. No sustained or long-term programmes were possible in its early years, only occasional seminars and an annual conference. There was certainly no money to interview 'ordinary' Coventry-based West Indians of the Windrush generation, but Professor Hennessy was adamant that the Centre would not be an elitist body, but would reach out to the modestly sized West Indian community, largely settled in the Hillfields area of Coventry.

I borrowed a tape recorder from the University's student radio studio, and through the West Indian Centre (a community social and recreational organisation), met some people who all declined to be interviewed, mainly because they were not comfortable being recorded. I suspect some had concerns about the legitimacy of their immigration status. Taking pity on me, the barman told me about an Indian-Guyanese man who lived the life of a hermit, rarely venturing out of his council flat. He was a neighbour of the barman's sister, who took pity on the lonely man and kept an eye out for him. He would not, however, receive charity, whether in goods or sentiment, and always strove to avoid the barman's sister. 'You is from BG [British Guiana], a coolie like him, maybe he'll gyaff [banter] with you,' the barman (African-Jamaican) said, with no hint whatsoever of racial intent. When I spent a little time in Jamaica, in 1984, I had experienced market vendors hailing strangers by their 'race': 'Black boy, how you doing?' 'Rastaman, buy something nuh?' 'Indian [sometimes, 'Coolie'], I get fresh tamarind just fuh you.' And, in truth, their address was not malevolent, for they gave each other nicknames, not just in Jamaica, but throughout the region. They identified each other by obvious features or ailments. A boy deprived of milk which caused his limbs to curve, they called 'Bowfoot'. Then there were 'Bruk Foot' (a man with a limp), 'Big Toe'(someone with huge feet), 'Black Jumbie' (a particularly dark-skinned fellow), 'Mad Rass' (someone suffering mental illness) and 'Godieman' (someone suffering from swollen testicles).

'In Demerara dem does call me "Turkey",' Mr Ram said, introducing himself. It was a sparsely furnished one-bedroom flat on the ground floor of a tower block. I had expected resistance when I rang the doorbell, but to my amazement he invited me in without enquiry as to my business. The barman's sister must have forewarned him and spoken kindly of me. I had also expected sullenness, or at best taciturnity, but Mr Ram startled me with his sense of humour. When I asked about the appellation, he burst out laughing, pointing to his face. 'You see how sharp my nose is, and my skull curve and flesh sag from me neck? From since I born, folk take one look at me and give me call-name. Black Turkey!' Was he pleased by his deformity, I wondered? After all, it marked him out, made him a recognised figure, even though of lowly status. I felt obliged to admire him, so I stared at his face for a short while before accepting his offer of tea.

* * *

Black Turkey (he insisted that I addressed him as such, possibly because it reminded him of village life back home) had come to Britain in 1950, at the age of 35. He was now approaching 70. He was born in 1915, two years before the system of indenture-ship was abolished by the British authorities in India. '"If you had" is what bring my father and mother to Demerara. They live their years by "if you had". So much so that when I was born they call me Ifwehad because I was all they had.' He stroked his head, remembering his parents. 'My birth-paper name is Ifwehad Ram! "Ifwehad" sound Hindi, no?'

It was so easy to converse with him; he wanted to talk and talk more. Was it because I was a fellow Indian-Guyanese, or because he took pity on me? I had told him I had left Guyana as a boy, in 1969, and never returned, so only had partial memories of the place.

'What work did your parents do in India?', I asked.

'Starve. That was their last calling in India. Before that they make and market fishnets, but drought come, trench turn mud, no fish. Nobody buy fishnet. So the only thing left to do is starve.'

I expected his voice to falter, but he leaned his head back to catch the sun struggling faintly through the front window and laughed. 'God called them to fishnet, then to starve, then to Demerara. One day a recruiter come to carry them away, the whole village,

and the next and the next. He had plenty food. They glad to ride
wagon through dust and animal bones. Then train take them on.
Month-end come, and there was the sea before them and the
waiting ship and stories about Demerara, how it get plenty gold.
And you know how coolie like gold! Bangle, hair-pin, nose-ring,
finger, gold!'

I had known, from books, something of the history of indentureship, but it was so much more beguiling hearing it 'live' from
Mr Ram. Shiploads fleeing famine. They would go anywhere, far
or near. To stay was to burrow for roots or to borrow money to
buy food, but the moneylenders' charges were so high, making
you pledge land, house, wife, young daughters, that it was cheaper
to starve, to outwait the sun. Rain did come, in the person of the
recruiter, who wanted nothing but little favours from the prettiest
wives. 'That is how I come to born, I not ashamed to say. My Pa
lolo [penis] shrivel, but recruiter eat plenty, his lolo stiff and cage
for woman.' He went on to divulge without pause the situation of
his parents, how his father, in return for a little money, accepted
that the recruiter had impregnated his wife, and was glad to leave
the village for Demerara. He never slept with her again since he
would not 'eat jutha'(following a Hindu practice of never partaking
of food left on anyone else's plate, deeming it to be tainted). She,
in turn, resented being soiled by the recruiter with her husband's
consent. She was determined never to sleep with him again. Mr
Ram was born soon after the landing, a child so dark-skinned
and distorted in appearance that his father was convinced that the
gods had put a curse on them. His mother thought he resembled
the recruiter, and vomited at the birth, just as she had after the
recruiter had dismounted her. 'I hear everything afterwards from
my mother, who loved me in spite of what happen to her in India.
When as a just-born baby I sob and wail and seek out her nipple,
she only remembering the wild noises the recruiter made when
he was on top of her, and his toothless gums. Even the village
midwife hurry off as soon as I drop.' They did not bother to call

a Hindu priest to perform the normal birth-ceremony. No invite
to neighbours to eat 'seven curry' (a festive dish made from seven
vegetables and served up on water lily leaves). Thus, Black Turkey
received no gifts. 'Not one rass bother to bless me when I born,' he
said in a matter-of-fact tone. 'Folk take one look at me and right
way know I is a bastard, I not resemble my father at all.'

For his first two years he was hidden away in the house, but he
learnt to walk. When his father went to work in the plantation's
punt gang or rat-poison gang, and when his mother went to the
trench to fetch water, Mr Ram would venture outside the hut and
frolic in the vegetable garden. The purple sheen of aubergines,
the feel of carilla (bitter melon) studs, the smell of ripe tomatoes,
these distracted him from his loneliness, he said, with no neighbours' children to play with. It was the beginning of his fascination
with and eventual marriage to the garden.

'I never like fruit. There was a mango tree in the yard. I used
to wonder whether my Pa and Ma break my legs to stop me leave
the hut, but it was the mango tree. There it was, yellowing with
fruit, tempting me to climb. Ma and Pa far. I climb it. Nasty tree!
It hide a bee nest so crafty that I didn't see it. The bees wait for
me to stretch out my hand for a mango, the tree sway deliberate to
stir them, I swear there was no breeze. The bees fly to my face, put
one sting on me! I tumble from the tree, break both legs. I walk
crooked ever since. I used to wonder whether Pa or Ma break my
legs out of spite or to hide me away, or if jaguar prowl the village,
then I will get catch and eat since I can't run. But it was the tree.
For years and years until I turn into a man, I suspect my Pa and
Ma for wickedness, but one day a man call Kukrit (they call him
so because he had a pointy head like kukrit palm seed) meet me
and tell me he see when I fall and how the bees shroud my face in
black. "It's true, blacker than even you! You turn black-black. And
you foot bruk. I see it. I was hurrying to market to sell plantain. I
was going to stop the cart, to see how you doing on the ground, I
but I was late so I just left you there. Somebody else would come

along and help, I think to myself, let me go and sell before market close." When Kukrit confessed, I didn't feel bad. He had to go to market to sell plantain, he had wife and pickni [children] to feed, what else he go do?'

* * *

I spent four sessions, about two hours each, taping Mr Ram. I assured him that if I published any part of the interview, I would change his name (hence, for the purposes of this chapter, I call him 'Mr Ram'). He was not worried that the interview would somehow reach Guyana: 'Dem all dead out, or migrate, the whole village, no one there to remember me. Still, just in case, don't name the village, just say "Demerara").' I wanted to spend much more time talking to him, but after the fourth meeting he changed his mind and closed up as suddenly as he had decided to engage with me that afternoon, a month before, when I plucked up courage to ring his doorbell − courage, because I thought I would be confronted by an eccentric hermit. I called upon him several times, but he didn't answer the doorbell. In my own words, mostly (Indian-Guyanese village creole, even when anglicised, can be hard to follow), the following is what I gathered from him in our all-too-brief encounter.

BG TO GB

Mr Ram's parents died young, of some tropical fever, but he was spared. It was a mere two weeks between his parents falling ill and dying. Mr Ram fed them water, since they could not stomach food, and they withered away. He was about 16, inheriting their mud hut, vegetable garden and mango tree. He lived on peas and aubergines, eaten with fish freshly caught in the village trench. He subsisted on this modest diet. His neighbours were charitable, providing salt, sugar and milk. His only companions, many years later, were two dogs, which, as puppies, were abandoned by the trench, and which he discovered on his way to fish.

War arrived in 1939, the British started to recruit young, strong Guyanese men to fight in France. Some hid for months in the jungle behind the village, thinking that they would be forced to enlist. 'A few men went off to fight, for the adventure. When the war done and they come back, they hop because they lose foot and leg. White man give them stilts, though. I had no worries the white people would want me. I walk crooked. Thank God for the bees and mango tree!'

One day, he returned from fishing to find his two faithful dogs were missing. Mr Ram was beside himself. The villagers had sighted a jaguar in the backdam. It was certain the jaguar had carried off the dogs. Once more, Mr Ram was alone.

Until Kukrit came. 'He say to me, your dogs gone, you can spend all your days eating fish and cabbage or you can come with me!'

Kukrit had decided that he wanted more than plantation work, and at weekends planting and selling vegetables. 'He hear that white people need hands in London to repair house and road that Germans bomb, plenty dollars, and only a little passage money.' Kukrit's plan was to work in London for a few years and send home money every month to feed his family. He would eventually send for them. 'In the meantime, he want me as a fellow traveller and will lend me the passage money. I was still pining for my dogs, I took one last look at the hut and the garden, and I say yes, leh we go!' That very afternoon they were in Georgetown, booked tickets, and boarded the ship a few days afterwards. Two weeks and a little more later, they emerged from their shared cabin to watch Tilbury approaching. A villager who had gone a year before met them, and found them a room and a paraffin heater in South London.

They easily found work at Lyons Corner House, washing dishes or undertaking simple tasks like peeling potatoes. The place was packed with West Indian workers. Mr Ram was content because it was still dark when he set off for the tube, and by the time he returned from work it was dark. Few saw him go and come, and the West Indians who practically filled the early morning carriages didn't bother to look at him, still awakening to daybreak. He wrapped a scarf around his face, not as protection against the black fog, but to aid invisibility. At work, the kitchen area, manned by West Indians, was a kind of sanctuary, further protecting him from the gaze of the white diners.

Kukrit was restless, though. He fretted that the wages were not rewarding enough. He thought of setting up a cook shop to cater for West Indians, but found out that a Jamaican had already done so, even arranging for peppers and salt fish and ground provisions (yam, cassava) to be shipped over from home. Plus, Kukrit didn't have enough to rent premises. He spent a lot of time thinking hard on how to make money. He made a compact with two Jamaican kitchen workers to hire a room in a cheap house and furnish it with a white girl, who would provide service to the wifeless and ravenous immigrants. A man from Barbados had begun such a venture in Brixton, so Kukrit took Mr Ram along on a reconnaissance mission to see how it was working. It was a Friday afternoon, so people had money in their pockets. There were five men lining the staircase leading to the room. They were waiting their turn, in the meantime sharing jokes, sharing stories about being in London, sharing news about their home island. The occasional groan from the room stilled them, but they quickly resumed their banter. When the client finished his business and made for the staircase, they would question him about value for money. His grin told them everything, the first in line quickly entered the room, and the men shuffled further up the stairs.

Kukrit also dropped this scheme. He said he was afraid of the police, he said fights might break out between one client and another if there was an attempt at jumping the queue, he said that men would want 'credit', promising to pay extra at month-end, but reneging on the promise, and they would get vexed when Kukrit declined their proposal. He was, after all, a slightly built

Indian, the clients were big and Black, by and large. They were bound to curse him and his race. Those were the reasons Kukrit gave when he dropped the plan to open up a mini-brothel, but Mr Ram believed it was because he remembered his wife and his two young daughters back in Demerara, and was full of remorse.

Food, sex and then death: Mr Ram's next plan was to open up a funeral parlour for Hindus. The bodies would be washed and anointed and garlanded with red flowers before being taken to the crematorium. 'No, no, no,' Kukrit said, scrubbing a frying pan with extra vigour. The plan would fail because it needed workers as well as a hearse and driver, and a supplier of coffins who would set up a credit line. 'Too complicated,' Kukrit told Mr Ram, but Mr Ram thought he was afraid of jumbies and hauntings, so withdrew.

They ended up in Coventry, because of the canal. Kukrit's paid job on the sugar plantation in Demerara was to clear the drainage canals of weeds and detritus. Waist deep in the water, with sack and shovel, braving snake and caiman, day after day, six of them. He loved his job once he got used to the work. To make the water flow more readily into the main canal which drained into the river and sea was a satisfying task. The sugar cane would rot without his efforts to clear the canals. So when he heard that Coventry was planning to restore its canal, he packed up his Lyons job and dragged Mr Ram to Coventry. 'London overrun with Jamaicans. You can't do new business,' he told Mr Ram. 'Coventry is new, we have not reached there yet, so we have space to prosper.'

When they got to Coventry, Mr Ram found kitchen work in a pub beside the canal, and stayed hidden from view for 30 years. He lived upstairs of the pub. Kukrit was taken on by the council, firstly to clean up the canal, but promotion was rapid since he took to the job like a duck to water. His employers rewarded his zeal by making him manager of a gang of Irish workers doing the cleaning up and the servicing of the locks. He ended up in charge of collecting fees for boats to moor. Within five years he made so much money that he returned to Guyana. In truth, he fled to

Guyana not only with his savings, but with a pile of mooring fees. He returned home on a BOAC (British Overseas Airways Corporation) airplane, not by boat. His departure was sudden, but he apologised for having to leave Mr Ram behind. 'I will set up a big cow business back home, I will send for you,' he promised. At first there was a monthly letter, but these got fewer and fewer, then dwindled to nothing. Mr Ram, when he retired from the pub's kitchen, was helped by the landlord to find a council flat. The landlord was so grateful for Mr Ram's work over so many years that he gave him a tidy sum of money. This, with his state pension, was sufficient to sustain him up to 1985, when I met him.

'Why didn't you go back to Demerara?', I once asked him. 'Nothing there for me. Nothing here for me. Best to stay where I am. Plus I got colour TV ....' He paused for a long while, thinking. 'Truth is, I miss planting carilla and aubergine and tomato and pumpkin ... and if I can cast my net in the trench water one last time, and pull up fish, but even if I don't pull up fish, just for one more time, then me done!'

3

From BG to GB

Elly Niland

All happy families are alike, but an unhappy family is unhappy after its own fashion.

(Leo Tolstoy, *Anna Karenina*, Penguin translation, 1954)

Travelling is a brutality. It forces you to trust strangers and to lose sight of all that familiar comfort of home and friends.

(Cesare Pavese)

I

It was the worst of times. A period of racial unrest, adding to uprisings and upheavals, began after Independence, when British Guiana was renamed the Republic of Guyana. The seeds of catastrophe were sown, and long lines of trucks carried armed militia through the country; there were murders, riots, rapes, racial strife and food shortages; disquiet spread like malarial mosquitoes. For seven months, radio broadcasts relayed the outbursts of violence countrywide. Then, after protests and petitions failed, the British troops arrived.

I guessed, years later, that in the midst of nationwide turmoil, my father had calculated the probability of a safe life under Forbes Burnham, the new dictator, and reached a poor prognosis. The only available serum was emigration.

Although memories discolour with age, this one revisits like a lingering ghost. It was a Wednesday when Mummy said, 'A letter came – your daddy in England wants you to live with him. No school today, we have things to do.' I looked at her, astonished. 'When? Why?' was all I could think to ask about this unexpected news. A vaccination for measles, a dental hygiene certificate and various other documents were required before I could cross the ocean to where the Queen and our rulers lived. A visit to the bank was necessary too, as I was allowed to leave with £5, the transaction officially stamped onto a page of my passport, which also stated that I was 4 feet 6½ inches tall and 13 years old. What a hectic time it must have been for mummy, with many other young children to care for, but the following week was full of excitement for me.

Even now, 53 years later, I remember my first ferry ride on the *Torani* with mummy. Its horn bellowed, it belched smoke. The race of water on the Berbice river was magical, and as it whipped up furious fans of foam, I could barely contain my rapture.

Figure 3.1 Elly Niland's passport photo at age 13, taken at the passport office in the Republic of Guyana on 27 November 1968. (Photograph courtesy of Elly Niland)

After collecting my visa from the British Embassy in Georgetown, we went to Booker stores, where green cloth for my dress,
orange cotton gloves, white slingback Cuban-heel shoes, a new
towel and a comb were bought for my trip. A pair of gold bangles
was a special gift from mummy. I marvelled at statues and traffic
lights and drank a whole bottle of Pepsi. It was the best of times.

But a young, gullible me never knew I would feel homesick,
never knew that after a wet-eyed departure from Atkinson
Airfield in Georgetown on board a Monarch airplane with a
pumpkin-coloured crown, I would spend so many years yearning
for my mother and my siblings. Or that this would be a voyage
without return. I knew only that I wanted to see my father, to call
him 'Daddy', and that I was going to live with him in England. I'd
witnessed him beating my mother, seen her lying helpless, bruised
and weeping. And yet, despite his mistreatment of us both, images
of his black-and-white brogue shoes, his shining Raleigh bicycle
and Wellington boots had not blurred. I loved him. He was the
handsome school headmaster whose hair and handwriting I
admired. I was sure to go on a red double-decker bus with him,
and I would see Buckingham Palace.

II

I arrived to a blizzard of unknown faces. Among the many things
which seemed strange to me, amidst the dense crowds and the
immense airport, was the worry that I had forgotten what my
daddy looked like. Somehow it seemed easier to picture a palace
and snow-covered holly trees with berries, but his face eluded me.
And his house was large, with carpet on every floor, somehow
eerie at first because I was used to the slap of feet on floors and
children beating up and down wooden steps, but here the people's
feet made no sound. A bathtub with hot running water was new
and fascinating. I now had a stepmother and three new siblings,
as well as my own room, with my own bed, and a desk and a

wardrobe. And the room was silent, except for a bubble of voices coming from the black-and-white television set downstairs, which became a consuming interest of mine. I found the advertisements especially entertaining.

There were many novelties to enjoy. Every Saturday night, my daddy made hotdogs with fried onions and Pepsi was served. On Sunday mornings, he'd cook breakfast and lunch, and would often invite friends to come over. I enjoyed adding sugar to my tea, and Carnation evaporated milk to my coffee, and I'd accompany daddy to the supermarket, and to the launderette. And in the cold, in the season of darkness, I saw newly naked trees, and it was fun to breathe through my nose and mouth at the same time, exhaling vapour.

Although homesickness was kicking in and I missed my best friend Margaret, school was safer at least. The only thing to sting my ears was the cold. There were no sharp tongues, no wild cane or painful ruler whacks on the knuckles when I was late, and no more sadistic schoolmasters when I did not satisfy some homework requirement or other. I no longer needed to fear authority, and I found some grit. However, my intellectual disability regarding numbers meant I sought to flee the intolerable mathematical monotony and the wall of thorns that was geometry, algebra and the rest. Indifferent to failure, I limped through lessons, dawdled between classes, and increasingly I began leaving school, sometimes visiting the library, window-shopping or roaming aimlessly. But my favourite place to skulk was always Tooting Market.

To a truant aged 15, the market teemed with life and laughter. I loved the cussing parrot, known as Mr Mack, who greeted customers with 'Pay me five bob' and 'Big batty boy'. I watched the pedlars, and entered bakeries and bookshops without challenge, even though I wore my school uniform. This bustling place was full of chaos and colour, it was like a balm. All of that and the calypso music added to the melody of rich, airy Caribbean voices. Apart from the feast for my eyes and ears, there was the scent of flowers, the aroma of sweetbread and seasoning and new hand-kerchiefs. I marvelled at the gaudy clothes on sale, and the noise of people higgling, or bartering, gave me a surge of contentment.

Letters from mummy would arrive, full of advice, but opening them was like reopening a wound. I was homesick, but I didn't know what for. Was it the longing for familiar things? The Indian films at the Gaiety Cinema or the sound of church bells? The sound of warm rain as it pelted on zinc rooftops and afterwards gleamed in puddles? Or the smell of fried callaloo and shrimps while Ma's pot spoon stirred and scraped the sides of her black cast iron karahi? I would wonder what time it was 5,000 miles away. I felt a longing, a raw pain that sharpened itself or became a dull hurt on certain dates, and tried to shake off the hollow feeling that I'd forgotten or lost something.

III

One year, ten months and three days after I left, another pale blue Par Avion letter from Mummy landed. I rubbed the edges. I had longed for it, yet also dreaded the news which transported me back to Guyana instantly. As I read, I could hear mummy's voice, and wondered if she was sweeping the yard or sifting rice right at that moment. She was always full of energy, always cleaning.

The shock when I read that almost every member of my family had scattered like rice grains across the Atlantic Ocean felt like a hit to the heart. The government body was stirring up bigger and better storms, and there was now a 'weekly exodus' from the country. Dispersal was speedy and secretive, entire families, two or three generations, extended family and friends, escaped. Some children were exported for their own safety with stickers on their chests declaring them 'unaccompanied minors'.

My grandparents watched as their six children, together with husbands and wives, departed to the United States of America, and every grandchild followed three weeks later. They had

Figure 3.2 Elly Niland aged 16, taken in London. (Photo courtesy of Elly Niland)

no family left except my mummy, who was planning to live in Canada. I wondered if they would recover from such wounds, and I thought about their sadness and the loss they must be feeling.

My younger sisters and brothers, who were not yet teenagers, had already left for North America, and I could only reach them in my head. I'd left with two gold bangles, but lost the jewels which were my family. That day, my endless wish to live again in Guyana dwindled to nothing, and I faced the fact that I was trapped in London with no hope of return.

IV

I met Chris on St Patrick's Day, in the Tara Dancehall, in Wimbledon, and that meeting would shape the next 50 years of our lives. We shared a penchant for pubs, and we would go to dances and cinemas too. He being from the west coast of Ireland and me being from Guyana, we had our differences. He preferred ice cream between two wafers, whereas I only ate the pink ones bought from Woolworths. But a fellowship grew based on childhood similarities: both born in our grandparents' house, both from tiny villages, both abandoned by our fathers, and our siblings were scattered, divided up and shared out among relatives. We also shared a history of colonial yokes. When I occasionally raised the lid of my Pandora's box, the scents of guava and sapodilla, the smell of hot dogs and the Berbice river seeped out. From his box came comic books, rabbits, football fields and incense, bulls' eye sweets, the smell of a turf fire, a drink of buttermilk and potato boxty, also called poor-house bread. Slowly, some of the mist that shrouded us lifted.

It was several years before we visited Ireland together, and Chris seemed queasy at the prospect. 'It's no *Tir Na Nog* [Land of the Fairies],' he said. We walked everywhere, and I tottered valiantly on platform shoes over untarred roads, up and down rough lanes, to visit his cousins of a similar age who spoke frankly about their schooldays, a time when they were made to interlace their fingers, palms downwards, before being whacked on the knuckles with a ruler. The eff word there was 'feck'. To be called an 'eejit' was rude, but a 'fecking eejit' was meant to sting. Phrases like '*póg mo thóin*' ('kiss my arse') peppered their tales, and 'Jazus, Mary an' Jozef' was exclaimed whenever there was news of a disaster or if you broke one of the 'good plates' or when a neighbour's young daughter was pregnant and unmarried.

I met the cousin who had placed him in a wheelbarrow and pushed him 4 miles from his grandparents' house in Dolan to Roundstone. She delivered him and his bottle of milk to the most loving aunt and uncle, who nurtured him for 14 years. She also explained that there was no hospital nearby, only a weekly bus, so if anyone due to deliver missed that bus, the baby was born at home. I heard from neighbours that his dog Sandy had been poisoned because it annoyed someone's sheep, and that he hunted rabbits and was envied by many children as he was the only one who owned a bicycle. One time, when we were helping to bring turf home from the bog, I was told that Chris's uncle used to place 'blasting caps', the detonators for dynamite, in some of the sods of turf, to deter people from stealing it. And Chris, being a curious child, had removed one and tried opening it with his teeth, but proving unsuccessful, he tried hitting it with a rock instead. As his aunt told me, he almost blew his own head off.

For me, these stories about him were like the missing pages of a book. Told in houses lit by lanterns and candles, some of the tales reminded me of home; children would rush indoors after dark, fearing banshees who lurked in the bushes. The same as in Guyana, I thought, though we called them 'Jumbies' We journeyed through history and mystery, and he told me of the time he stood on a friend's shoulders to steal apples from the monastery garden, but fell from the high red brick wall, breaking his arm. At home, he was in pain but refused to explain his injury, so the Garda was called because his aunt feared that someone had hurt him intentionally. He confessed his crime, was driven 60 miles to the hospital in Galway, and returned with a plaster. So ended his career as a robber, but to his friends he returned a hero.

The Dolans, the Diamonds and the Keaneys were unfailingly kind and indescribably entertaining. 'Welcome to Ireland,' they'd say, and walking over to shake Chris's hand, they'd ask if I spoke English, and when he said 'yes,' they'd shake my hand too. '*Céad mìle fáilte* [a hundred thousand welcomes].' 'Have yourself a grand time, the sun is due out any day.' I loved Lough Corrib red lemonade, Tayto crisps, Galtee and Calvita cheese, Boland's Kimberley and Mikado biscuits, known as Mickeydoos. I feasted on Donnelly's sausages, white pudding, floury potatoes dug just before meals, warm soda bread and barm brack, not to mention the blessed trinity of Jameson's, Bushmills and John Powers whiskey. Tomato juice with vodka, salt and Worcestershire sauce was called a 'Bloody Mary'. Tomato juice without vodka but with herbs was called a 'Virgin Mary'. Plain tomato juice was a 'Bloody Shame'.

But Chris was right, it wasn't all fairies, and I learnt about the priests and the nuns, those brutal sadists, practised paedophiles, womanisers and alcoholics. Surely now everyone has heard about the horrors, and how the Church used fear and shame and ignorance to exploit adults and children alike. Both Chris and his sister Ann had their years of cruelty and neglect at the hands of the un-Christian Brothers, and the Sisters Without Mercy.

I only tasted the ignorance, which came first when sitting with my mother-in-law, near Gurteen Beach one day. By the rockpools which Chris had often spoken about, and which our son Philip would love, a well-upholstered woman with brows drawn together called out, 'How are ye Maggie?' Her skirt was the shade of unripe tomatoes, and her hair blowing in the wind reminded me of froth in a pot when rice was about to boil over. 'So you brought over the Injan from Amerikay.' She peered, stretched her neck and tilted her head at me. 'Almost the same as Smithwick's Ale.' I moved a short distance away to collect pebbles with Philip, but still heard snatches. 'Maggie, does that one know anythin' what we're sayin' at all?' Two parallel furrows across her forehead deepened, 'Jes tell me now, Maggie, how will the child understand what she says? And how will she know what he wants, eeh? God help the poor mixi lad.' My mother-in-law didn't come to my defence, rather, she knotted her face and clenched, then made verbal ash of her son's wife.

And there were more like them, their words slithering out. They'd talk about me, but never to me. Odd that it was so difficult for them to address me when I was present, but they were somehow able to address an absent God. I was of another race and looked unlike anyone in the whole village, and with my 2½-inch platform soles and my garish clothes, some comments were to be expected. But the rawness of their sub-standard words was hurtful. Perhaps I should have discharged some succulent Creole in return, but in an ambush of stares, I'd smile indulgently instead.

It wasn't just the Irish or the village folk, of course. Back in London, when a janitor answered the door, eyes crawling all over me, he gave a short laugh and shouted, 'Paddy, there's a coon bird 'ere askin for yuh.' Men in pubs with belts straining under their paunch: 'Got nothing against them, but you should marry your own kind.' People often spat 'Paki-lover' at Chris. Waiting at the pedestrian crossing, a woman asked if she could just touch me for good luck as she was going to bingo. And in Mothercare, a middle-aged woman seemed to be admiring my baby until she pronounced, 'His dad not your kind, then?'

Despite the reptilian priests, the comments about chessboard babies and zebra babies, I was determined to return to Ireland every year so my children could see that magnificent mountain range and live in that landscape, climb Eris Beg and visit the Aran Islands. I would buy them a *bodhrán* and a tin whistle, whether they played them or not. We would take home the turf, we would visit the Dolans, the Diamonds and the Keaneys, we would go to weddings and funerals, and we would belong.

4

Made through Movement

Nalini Mohabir

Sailing from Port of Spain to Southampton, she stands alone at the docks, suitcase in hand. In Trinidad, she is a salesperson. In Britain, she will train to be a nurse. A subsequent migration to Canada, however, means that the career proves elusive. Qualifications not recognised as a result of crossing an ocean, she will become a retail worker yet again.

Hundreds of Caribbean women made momentous journeys during the middle decades of the twentieth century from places deemed small-ish. But what do maps know? You have seen these women, in their worn coats and black orthopaedic shoes, plastic bags at their feet, standing on a subway platform in London, New York or Toronto.[1] They are on their way home after another long shift in a service industry (retail? food? homecare?). This is my mother's story of migration from Trinidad to England to Canada, entwined with my father's, my auntie's and mine. What follows is a brief reflection on an interview I conducted with my parents, and then the interview itself about my parents' Windrush-era migration from the Caribbean to the UK, or rather how they recount their memories of migration to me, their daughter.

My mother's hands are an ocean – but only a generation – away from hard work in the fields, unlike me, whose only 'field work' has been that of academic tourism and travel to archives. I first interviewed my mother for a stage production at Leeds a decade

---

1 With inspiration from and thanks to the poem 'The Emigrants' by Kamau Brathwaite (1967).

ago. Produced by Carol Marie Webster, the piece was entitled *Mother Libation* in commemoration of mothering in the African Diaspora. My inclusion in this kind of production is perhaps only possible in the UK, a site where ex-colonials encounter each other and creolisation takes on the form of political Blackness. I was also asked to participate as someone of Indian-Caribbean descent, because we have been positioned in relation to African-Caribbean experiences since our arrival in the region. We come to know ourselves through the complexity of stories emanating from the womb of the Caribbean and her diaspora.

My mother's story was not easy to come by, as it emerged slowly on a need-to-know basis, as in: 'Child, why you ask me that?' I was first motivated because I wanted to know more about her relationship with Auntie Myrtle, a friendship sustained across borders for over 50 years. Each year, without fail, Auntie Myrtle posts Christmas presents from London: socks and scarves from Marks & Spencer for me, tea and biscuits for my parents. When I moved from Toronto to Leeds to pursue graduate studies, my mother informed me that Auntie Myrtle would be my 'mom away from home', and she was.

My mom, Amiran, grew up in the south of Trinidad (Siparia), where she went to a school run by Canadian Presbyterian missionaries. Since she was Muslim, she also attended the masjid and received Arabic lessons, but her parents made sure she went to other religious services too. The daily lived experience of creolisation (of 'intermixture and enrichment') in Trinidad meant she also attended the Pentecostal church, Spiritual Baptist ceremonies and the Hindu mandir.[2] Trinidad might be a small island, but it contained a world. In 1965, at the age of 25, her world widened. She stood at the docks of Port of Spain, with carloads of family, aunts, uncles, brothers, sisters, cousins, nieces and nephews who

2   See Kamau Brathwaite, *Contradictory Omens: Cultural Diversity and Integration in the Caribbean* (1974; reprinted Mona, Jamaica: Savacou Publications, 1985), p. 11.

47

had travelled from all corners of the island to say farewell, perhaps sensing her departure would be without a return. My older cousin told me that as a young girl, her dreams expanded thanks to seeing my mother board the ship alone. Mom was the first to leave Trinidad. Like many women from the Caribbean, marriage and work wasn't an either/or choice, and her aspirations weren't confined to wife or mother. She was leaving to seek an education and career in England. She broadened all our horizons.

When my mother arrived in England, the hospital was supposed to send someone to pick her up, but they forgot about her. So she hitched a ride with an ambulance. The matron was apologetic, and offered my mom – who had been travelling all day on an empty stomach – pork and beans. Luckily, before any unease set in, she met Auntie Myrtle. Myrtle was my mother's nursing college room-mate, and they shared a sparse room with two beds in the dorm. Myrtle had arrived three years earlier from Barbados, and had an older sister in London who provided a nurturing lifeline of pepper sauce, plantain, peas and rice, delivered on the weekends to Auntie Myrtle and mom. I have a feeling this made up for the pork.

Myrtle taught my mom and her fellow nurses from the Caribbean how to shop, travel, and negotiate freedoms and restrictions in this new space. The four women in Figure 4.1, from Barbados, Grenada, Trinidad and Jamaica, were part of a workforce of colonials and ex-colonials invited to work in Britain, but who nevertheless were racialised as migrant workers, needing their visa renewed every six months. They overcame obstacles through a sort of communal defence, fortified by friendship. Plus they knew how hard each other had to work to achieve their dreams. But how did they not only survive, but thrive? Well, they found time to be young and alive, to date, to dress up, to sip tea like Caribbean queens at Harrods (and, I imagine, to dance … not necessarily to the Mighty Sparrow, but a l'il wine to Tom Jones, The Beatles or whatever else moved the dance clubs of Reading).

But most of all, they survived through the lessons learned in the Caribbean about solidarity, kinship and living with difference. In 1968, all four women pictured received their State Enrolled Nursing Certificate.

Figure 4.1 Myrtle (first left) with Nalini Mohabir's mother Amiran (third left). (Photo courtesy of Nalini Mohabir)

For my father, Avin, whose story is recounted briefly in Parts II and III of the interview, we have a differently gendered perspective on the challenges of trying to settle in London, although in his narrative, even the name-calling, threats of violence and hesitant friendships are scrubbed clean, possibly to keep a space of hope alive for a world that might be otherwise.

As much as I want to believe in the otherwise of a utopian multiculturalism, these interviews with my parents do not suggest that their generation became a foundation of multicultural Britain, rather it shows that the Windrush generation was made in movement. The Windrush detentions and deportations, on the other hand, demonstrate the state's fixity on un-belonging, particularly towards African-Caribbean people. The Windrush scandal was further exacerbated by a rush towards white innocence disguised by seemingly neutral definitions of home bordered by the Home Office and the Home Secretary. But home was never neutral. For those whose passports marked their expansive national status as 'British Subject Citizen of the United Kingdom and Colonies', the roots of the Windrush scandal were unmistakably colonial, connected to the end of British subjecthood and the denial of substantive British citizenship, entangled with shifting ideas of home and homeland in flux during decolonisation. In particular, my father's narrative suggests the pains of coming to terms with this history and memory for 'double migrants', those who migrated from the Caribbean to England, and then left, either to Canada or the United States, but not to settle. No, these individuals were un-settlers, unsettled by processes set in motion through hundreds of years of colonialism, an unsettling that for many of us continues in the present.

PART I: MOM CARRIED HER HOME IN A SUITCASE

Nalini: You went to England as part of the Windrush generation, did you feel compelled to leave Trinidad to have a future?
Mom: My father died when I was young, I left school at 12. My father used to build houses, but people wouldn't pay him, instead they would give him rum. And my mom used to go to people's houses to cook, before that she picked tonka beans. There wasn't a high school in Siparia, and we didn't have money to pay for higher education in San Fernando or Port of Spain, so I started working as a salesperson.[3] I tried to write exams to get a scholarship for high school, but they said I was too old and wouldn't let me. I feel it was because I was poor. I wasn't getting no chance.

A lot of people didn't go to high school in those days. Most of the friends I grew up with got married soon after leaving school. They were Hindus and had arranged marriages.

---

3   The first high school in Siparia, Trinidad was Iere High School, founded in 1955.

I tried to get into the nursing programme in San Fernando, but we had no connections. So I had to make it on my own. I thought, 'Well, if I could go to England, I would be able to do something with my life.'

N: How did you find out that they were looking for nurses in England?

M: I took my mom to the doctor, Dr Sampath's office in Siparia, and there I saw a newspaper. There was an ad in the newspaper; I copied the address, and wrote to Reading Group Hospital. They wanted nurses to come and work in England, and they would train you and pay you a small salary. That was 1964. I was 24 years old

N: What did the ad say they were looking for?

M: They didn't list any qualifications. You had to do an interview and pass an English test and an oral test. The people from England came to interview us in Trinidad. They didn't ask biology questions. They just asked me what I do, where I work, and why I want to go. I told them I want to further my studies and be a nurse.

N: What made you want to be a nurse?

M: I always see the old people who go to the DMO [District Medical Officer]. They had to line up – in long lines – because there was not much help.

N: Since you left after Independence, would you have travelled on a Trinidadian passport?

M: Yes. I had to turn in my British passport and coordinate my Trinidad passport, birth certificate, an affidavit, as well as a visa from England and a letter from the hospital. Everyone thought I was crazy – even to this day – my brother asked me how I knew to do all the paperwork! I had to educate myself.

On the day my mother died, the letter from England came for me, and when it came, I made up my mind to leave. I was too ambitious to know what I was doing. And I loved school.

N: What did the letter say?

M: They promised me a place to live, meals would be provided, uniforms would be provided, and you'll get schooling.

N: What did you know about England growing up?

M: When I was a kid, you would see the royal family visit. You would have to have your uniform all pressed and ironed and line up in the hot sun to wave a flag to the royal people. That's all I knew.

N: How did you prepare to go to England?

M: I took a car from San Fernando to Port of Spain. You know, we had big European stores in Port of Spain? I went to Fogarty's and asked the clerk what I needed. Everyone was giving me a little hint – it's cold. My sister was so worried that she sewed a suit and lined it with flannel for me because she said I don't know where I'm going. It was a lovely suit, like a real professional, with white gloves like the ones you see in [Andrea Levy's] *Small Island*.

N: Tell me about the day that you were leaving Trinidad.

M: I left by boat. I couldn't afford a plane ticket because I was carrying my own expenses. It cost me $300.

The ship was bigger than I thought, I could barely walk up because the wind was high. And all my relatives and all my co-workers came to see me off. It was a very happy moment. Everyone was clapping for me. It was a big deal because in those days not a lot of Indians would send their girl child overseas. The name of the ship was the *Pinta*, and it took three weeks to reach Southampton. The only cabin I could afford was a cabin shared with six girls, mostly Portuguese. It was good in one way, because you would look out for each other when you go to the shower and thing.

I arrived in January 1965. From Southampton, they put us on the train. And when I reached London, I had to find the right platform for Reading. So I looked for signs, and then people direct you. Jamaicans were very nice. Jamaicans were the ones who used to run the trains and do the porter work. And when they see Caribbean people, they treat them like a queen! They were so happy to see somebody from the Caribbean islands! And I could speak too! Because, you know, in those days, people were still very prejudiced.

So they put me on the right train. I had to get to Henley-on-Thames, and when I reach there, it was late at night, the trains stopped running, and I had two suitcases with me. Luckily, I had a coat, twice the size of me.

The hospital was supposed to send someone to meet me. So I waited. An ambulance driver saw me walking up and down, up and down. And he read the label on my suitcase. He said, 'Buses don't run at this time of the night, I am going to take you to the matron.' The matron got up. She went and get a room for me. She said they were expecting me, but they didn't have the date – which I think was a big lie. The first thing she asked me was if I had eaten, and I said, no. So she gave me baked beans and sausages, which I never ate because I'm Muslim. But I was happy to get a cup of tea. That was my first introduction to English food (laughing).

My room was nice. I had a lock and a key. There were two single beds. I preferred to share, because if you share, one girl can look after the other. So that's how I met your Auntie Myrtle [from Barbados], we shared a room. Myrtle told me how things worked in England. I had a bank draft to cash, and she took me to the bank. You couldn't trust any and anybody to do things for you, but I trusted her. Without her, I wouldn't have been able to survive. She's very smart, you know, she's related to the Barrows [Errol Barrow was the first Prime Minister of Barbados]? She knew how the system worked. I came from Siparia, so I wasn't as exposed to the world like her.

The next day, I had to go to the matron's office, take my passport, my birth certificate, my visa, all my documents for her to look at. She said, 'We're not going to keep this, but we have to send it to head office to have it approved.' And after a few days, I got it back, and that was it.

N: What was your training like?

M: I worked as an orderly until classes started. There were many nurses from the Caribbean: Jamaica, Barbados, Grenada, Antigua. Your Auntie Myrtle was in my class. There were some from Nigeria, and the rest from Wales and Scotland. They were stuck up. All the whites sat one side, and the coloured people sat on the other side. They work you hard, and you're so tired. You have to work on the wards, and then go to class, and then after class, study. They told me I would never pass. For the final exams, everybody was studying, studying, but Myrtle and I would still go out. We would go to the big stores like Harrods. Myrtle said if the Queen could eat those fancy things, we could eat it too! So we would dress up better than the English people and go to Harrods, even if all we could afford was a cookie or a cup of tea.

N: Did you meet any Indian-Caribbeans training to be nurses?

M: There weren't very many, and they didn't treat me nice. When they invited me to their home, I would take Myrtle with me. And it was like they shun us, like they don't like Black people. I walked away. I wasn't going out without Myrtle, so I never went back.

There were a few nurses from India, but I couldn't understand when they speak, and then they wanted to sell me sarees. I don't know to wrap them things.

I keep together with the Jamaicans, they were friendly and outgoing, and with Myrtle and her sisters.

N: Did you think that you were going to stay in England? Or did you plan to come back to Trinidad?

M: No, I couldn't go back to Trinidad because there was nothing there for me. Where you get money to feed everybody? To pay school fees for nieces and nephews? I was constantly struggling.

N: How did the patients in England treat you?

M: Nice. They love to hear my [Trinidadian] voice. One man used to say I have such a beautiful sing-song voice he's not sick any more. They used to ask for me.

N: What did you do on your days off?

M: You know, you're from the islands, you're not used to this island. When we know somebody was coming, we'd go to London, to the train station or the airport. We would look to see where the West Indian people were, just to feel a part of life.

I met your dad's cousin at the airport. I don't know how Myrtle and I end up at the airport but I saw someone holding up a sign with your dad's name. I recognised the name because your father and I were pen pals for many years [he lived in British Guiana]. I gave his cousin my phone number to pass to your dad. Because we had written to each other for so long, I thought at least I'll have somebody to communicate with. And thank goodness, because nobody from Trinidad wrote to me.

He would come up to Henley-on-Thames and we would take a walk or we would go to London and visit the museums or gardens because they're free, and then he would bring me back home.

PART II: CURRY STAINS AND BITTER OLIVES   DAD

Nalini: Why did you leave Guyana? What was your arrival in England like?
Dad: I came to England to study radio and television. Television was the future, and there were no TVs in Berbice. I was ahead of my time.

There was one man from Yorkshire, a former journalist, who used to work at Albion Sugar Estate [Guyana], and he would tutor me. I was the first non-white person to be invited into one of the estate homes at Albion.

I left Georgetown in 1965. I didn't know if I was coming back. Because of the race riots and politics in Guyana, everyone was telling me, 'Go, don't come back.'

I left on a BOAC [British Overseas Airways Corporation] plane, which flew to Barbados, then Bermuda, then to Heathrow. I was dressed in a blue suit made by tailor Jeff and had a colonial passport. The passengers were mostly white folks, and there was a white man sitting beside me. And of course, when they served the meals, I see trouble. I don't know about knife and fork, I always used to eat with my hand. It was a bit difficult. They also gave us olives, but I didn't know what it was. It didn't have a sweet taste, and I couldn't swallow it. So I just spit it out and put it in my back pocket. I didn't learn about olives till I reached England and saw it in the stores.

Your Uncle Polo was waiting for me at the airport. He told me someone was there to see me. I stayed with Uncle Polo and two other guys in a rooming house. I shared a room with his brother. We were all working or going to school. I had to learn how to cook, iron, wash dishes, mend clothes.

N: Did you experience racism in England?

D: Well, people call you names, but I didn't really pay attention.

I was told not to go on the train when there's a football match, because you could get beaten. I avoided the train during those times. Anyway, it was much worse in Canada. I found more prejudice in Canada than I ever found in England.

In London, I was made supervisor at Coxhead Rentals [a TV rental store], but a white employee said plain, 'I'm not working under you.' I said, 'Fine, you can leave.' Another time, a man, he was in the army, came in and shouted at me, but I didn't let it bother me. When I first went to a white friend's home, his wife said, 'Why did you bring this man here?' But she was nice, I even slept in their house, in the corridor.

I made friends with guys from Nigeria and Singapore. Indians used to bring their TVs to me to fix, although some would stop talking to me because I didn't know Hindi. If you're Indian from another part of the world, some of them don't want to know you.

PART III: FROM ENGLAND TO CANADA

Nalini: Did any immigration issues come up?

Mom: Things start changing in England. A lot of the girls [nurses] didn't get their stamps renewed in their passports. I don't know why. Your dad's visa expired in 1968, and they would not renew it for him, so he went to Canada.

N: Why did you leave England to go to Canada?

Dad: After Guyana became independent, they [the British] wouldn't renew my visa. I didn't want to quarrel with them because I wasn't sure how things worked in England. Anyway, money was running out, so I tried Canada. This time, I was travelling on a Guyanese passport. I went to the Canadian High Commission, and they said I had enough points, I could immigrate.[4] So then Mom and I got engaged. I told her I would go get a job and a flat in Canada and come back for her. Whether she believed me or not, I don't know.

In 1969, I came back, and we got married at City Hall, and left England the next day because your mom's visa was about to expire. I won some money in the football pool, so from there, we went to Trinidad to have a Muslim wedding, then a Hindu ceremony in Guyana, and then we came to Canada. They gave us champagne on the plane because we were newlyweds (laughing).

M: For me, every time I have to get my visa extended, I have to give these white people [the matron] my passport, and they send it away. Why can't I send it myself? What is this?

Plus Canada was offering settlement to people from Britain – you come here and help and build the country. That's how we come in 1969. They didn't like people from the Caribbean at that time, a lot of people had to come here illegally. But they let us in because they were taking people direct from England.

D: I wonder what would have happened if we stayed.

Looking back, it's very nasty the way the UK treated the Windrush people, as if West Indians were not members of the British Commonwealth, as if we had no connection, as if we were not invited to work. West Indian people did so much for the

4   The year before, in 1967, Canada removed overt race-based criteria for immigrants and instituted a points system to select immigrants.

Empire, and for the Crown. They should have found a way for all of us to stay in England. The English couldn't even build a toilet, but when the Windrush generation came, they built good houses and built up neighbourhoods no one wanted.

The Windrush deportations should never have happened, especially after so many years. Did they consider Irish foreigners and deport them? The British have never been fair.

* * *

My parents give me this story of a time I did not know.
Sometimes home is getting away
and finding something to hang onto.

(Nalini Mohabir)

5

Interview: 'Trinidad Implants in you this Wonderful Sense of Carnival'

Bob Ramdhanie

This is an oral history interview with Dr Bob Ramdhanie MBE, conducted by Maria del Pilar Kaladeen on 5 January 2021.

Bob, I wondered, first of all, how old you were when you came here?

I was just over 17, I had finished O-levels, which in those days we had in Trinidad. When I finished, my brother said to me: 'You'll be going to college in England in August to study electrical engineering.' I joked to myself, 'I can't even *spell* electrical engineering! Where has this come from? Nobody in my life had ever asked me what I want to do, and now you're telling me as a young man I'm going to England?' But I think the second reason was, having had two deaths in the family and having a sister who was already in London and a brother who was already in London, there being four of us, he said, 'You're going to join your brother and sister.'

So I came here totally, *totally* bewildered, and in those days, very much like the *Windrush*, I came on a boat that took 14 days, possibly 11 of which were spent sharing what went into my tummy with either my room-mate (vomiting in the sink!) or the fishes. I was sick like a dog! That was 1965. If you can imagine, coming from a tiny village in Trinidad where I was born, in Claxton Bay, everyone in the village are your uncles and aunties – most of my uncles and aunties were from Grenada, of course they were living in Trinidad – and other Trinis. We had this sense of community. Of course, we had fracas if somebody had too much rum, or little boys playing cricket – that could get heated. Or we had a card game called 'All Fours', and that's where you saw the passion of Trinidadians. Calypso music, cricket, food, socialising was a big thing amongst people, and of course church. All of these things blended into one another. I never had a vision of what this big wide world was. By the time I was coming to England, I had lived in San Fernando, I had spent a lot of time in Port of Spain, where my cousins were, I was a little bit worldly in a Trinidadian context. I say that in the context that I had been to Queen's Hall, I had been to public concerts, I'd seen Miriam Makeba perform, I'd been to the theatre, I was in my school carnival band, I was in my scout group, as opposed to being a little village boy who had never left his village. But even all of that was no preparation for being in a place like London in 1965, it was just ultra-amazing.

When you first arrived, where did you go?

I had a sister and a brother here, I landed … it must have been Southampton, and we got a train to Waterloo, I think it would have been, and the first thing that struck me was that my brother had a tie on, with a jacket that looked like it was four times smaller than his size, with chequered trousers. He was a couple of years older than me. He's now passed away. We would go to church together, and this sort of Caribbean thing we had that church clothes were white shirts and black trousers. Everything was dark and dowdy, because I think that's the way that we believed the Lord wanted us to be! The way he was dressed, I was like, 'What the hell is wrong with you?!' And then he looked at me in my slim-fitting trousers that were cut way above the ankles so you could see my red socks, which was very trendy in Trinidad – skinny, I was! And he looked at me like, 'What a mess!'

The interesting thing was on the boat, Cecil Parkes, an Afro brother – now, I'm saying 'Afro brother' because today there's a context, but in those days, he was a Trini – he was coming here to join the Army, and we became friends on the boat. So when we're getting in to Southampton, he said to me, 'You know, I'm coming up here to join the Army,' that was still for another four weeks, 'and I have nowhere to stay,' and I said, 'No problem, no problem, come and stay with us,' not having a clue where I'm going! When my sister came, I said, 'Sis, Cecil, who's a good friend of mine, has nowhere to go for the next four weeks, can he stay by us?' She said to me, 'Well, I've got you a room with a single bed in it, and that's it.' And I just thought – again, the brain is completely Trinidadian – 'That's great, we throw something on the bed, and he sleeps with us.' My sister had made curry, roti, dahl, so there was home food.

My first shock was when we came to 19 Crockerton Road in London, SW12 or SW17, I think, and we came in, went upstairs, and my sister went to the right and she pointed me to the left on this landing. I said, 'Oh.' She went to her room on this landing and I went to mine, and on the middle of this landing there was the shower at the front, and at the back of the rooms was the kitchen. Here was me thinking, 'Oh sis, this is a nice little place you've got,' not realising there are Nigerians living upstairs, English people living downstairs, so we all had 'rooms'. So my first few days, I was sharing my space with somebody I just met on the boat, who now ... that was 1965, we're now in 2021, and we've remained close friends. He now lives in Canada, and he calls me every single week. Every Sunday, he calls me.

That's a 55-year friendship!

I also said to him, 'The Army is not for people like you, Cec, come on, maybe if you came to join the services, you had to ... but join the Air Force, become a mechanic or an engineer, do something that pushes you up the scale.' At the time, also my brother was in the Royal Marines, and my best friend from school in Trinidad was already in the UK, in the Army, and was based in Germany. So, you can imagine, four guys meeting at my place when they had leave, all four of us slept in that same room, all four of us ate in that same room! We had this one paraffin heater that we all warmed ourselves from. We had Army, Air Force, Marines, and they were like: 'Okay, Robbie, you just read your books, we'll do the real jobs!'

My sister was a nurse, her boyfriend at the time, now her husband, is a Barbadian, and he was doing psychiatric nursing, and all the people that my sister knew, white, Black, English, Irish, Caribbean, were all doing nursing. There was a kind of fraternity that I met through my sister, and really in those days, as you said, we certainly felt we belonged, but we also knew that we were viewed through different lenses. There was a fantastic sense of community among the Caribbean people we knew. And remember, nurses came from all over the Caribbean, so you weren't only meeting Trinis, you were meeting Jamaicans, Barbadians, Antiguans, Guyanese, Kittitians and both male and female nurses, because England was advertising in the Caribbean for nurses, that was a passport up to the UK in those days. Since 1962, with all the immigration restrictions, you had to be coming here with purpose, so a lot of them came via the nursing profession, the NHS.

If you went to a party (and we had a lot of house parties in those days, we weren't into clubs and all that sort of stuff), there was that kind of code of belonging to a community. We picked up in the Irish pubs that if you happen to dance with a white person you can feel the tensions rising, so we always had a lot of home parties where there were people like us, including a lot of English men and women who were nurses, so there was a fraternity.

The wonderful thing about immigrants in those days is that when they met you for the first time, even before they asked your

name, the question is: 'How long have you been here?' And that is
because they had this pecking order, but more importantly, those
who had been here four or five years before you would take you
under their wings. We had this real built-in infrastructure, where
Trinis, Jamaicans, Guyanese who were here before you kind of
coached you to fit in.

It was a wonderfully strong unit. The Jamaicans, Antiguans and
Kittitians who had come to do nursing, a lot of them also came
and were carpenters and working on the trains, whereas a lot of
the Trinis and Guyanese, we were here as students. If we weren't
nurses, most of us were in college or university. Weekends were
when we got together, and we had identified a pub, an Irish pub
in London where we'd gather. There'd be steel band and calypso,
there was a woman who used to sell roti, so that all those connections in those early years were about Caribbean identity.

We never chatted about racism in those days. Never discussed
it, but you were conscious of it. But certainly, late 60s, early 70s,
you began to feel it – when there were more immigrants coming
in since the *Windrush* – British subjects from all over the world.
I'm not even talking about the Enoch Powells of this world – you
as an individual. I would get on the buses and folks would put
their bags on the bus or the tube so I wouldn't sit next to them,
and I would go home and cry. People would call me 'wog'. The
first time I was called a wog or a paki, I didn't know what it meant.
So I would go home and say to my sis: 'I was called a wog today,
what's that?' She was always so protective. She always had a way of
coping. But as a Trini and with other Caribbean friends, we were
not a 'Who am I?' people. We knew who we were. We were really
strong Caribbean Black people. All of us were Black in those days.
We never spoke about Indians or South Asians in the 60s and the
70s. In those days, when I was growing up, I was campaigning on
the streets in London, and when I was the President of Leicester
Polytechnic Students Union or later working for the Probation
Service in Birmingham, we were all Black people.

Did those experiences of racism you had in London, did they motivate you to become political, to become involved in politics at university, to work in the Probation Service in Birmingham – to try to make things more equal, less painful, for others?

To be honest, when I came, I went to a private school in London – as I said. my brother put me on this path to become an electrical engineer. He sent me to a private school, Pembridge College of Electronics, which was in Bayswater, London. So, I came there, and I did City and Guilds. Then, when I finished, I went to Wimbledon Tech and I did an OND [Ordinary National Diploma] in engineering, and then I went to Leicester Polytechnic to do an engineering degree. But by the time I was at Wimbledon College, I had found myself a Saturday job, so I was getting to understand the system etcetera … I then took the liberty of saying to my older brother in Trinidad who had sent me to England, when I graduated from Leicester, 'Well, thank you very much, I've satisfied the family, you wanted me to train as an engineer, I've trained as an engineer.' Nowhere in my heart was there a space for engineering, and that was the truth. And then I reflected, 'What do I really want to do?'

It wasn't England's society *per se* that put me on this road, but I always wanted to be a minister in my Church, in the Presbyterian Church. So I thought, 'Now I've done my family thing, I've graduated as an engineer, great, I can do what I want.' My sister had long left and gone to Canada. My brother was still here, living in Essex. I thought, 'Well, Bob, you're on your own.' I thought about studying theology to satisfy what I wanted to do. I was chatting to some friends, and one said, 'Bob, are you sure about Theology? If you want to help people, why don't you go and do social work?' Well, when you came from the Caribbean in those days, there were only four professions you know? All of your family and friends – doctors, lawyers, accountants and engineers. And then I discovered things like archaeology, and I thought,

'God! This is so interesting.' I started looking at history. But this person said social work, and I thought maybe that's one way I could help people.

I did a Master's in Social Work at Leicester University, and I chose, before the course was finished, to look at joining the Probation Service rather than Social Services. By then I knew, I was wise enough to know, that there were many more Blacks in the prison systems as a percentage than there were per our numbers in society. So it was prior to even going to university I had this notion of Black people – and by Black, as I said, I mean all non-whites – in this political context, all of us who were oppressed, were Black people. I was going to Black Panther meetings in Leicester even before I went to university.

When I was in Leicester, I was volunteering, I was 'teaching' kids after-school sessions in a primary school where the head teacher was Mr Robinson, a fellow Caribbean. When I was doing my probation training, I would go back in on Saturdays and Sundays to the local borstal where I was on secondment, above and beyond my training hours, and work with some of the youths who were mostly Black – there were some white youngsters who would come too. I would get them to write about their experiences, and I would create little plays and that sort of stuff. I was always trying to engage them in ways for them to express who they were and how they were feeling!

How did you end up in Birmingham from Leicester?

I started to scout around before I graduated, and as it happened, an Acting Chief Probation Officer [ACPO] in Leicester had then moved and become the Chief Probation Officer in Birmingham. I did my probation training period in the Leicester Probation Service, so somebody must have thought I was not too bad because I got a letter from the Chief who had moved from Leicester asking me to consider coming to have a look in Birmingham when I graduated. I thought, 'Hmmm.' Birmingham was never on the horizon, it was always back to London for me. I started reading up about Birmingham, and there were a couple of Brummies on the course who said to me, 'If you go to Birmingham, don't go to Handsworth, don't go to Aston,' and I thought, 'Why?' These were, of course, white students. So I started reading about Handsworth and the Black communities there, and I said to my wife, 'That's where we're heading. I want to work in Handsworth. Not only do I want to work in Handsworth, but I think that's where we should live.' I accepted a post in Birmingham.

When I worked in Birmingham, I was based in Perry Barr, and the office is spitting distance from the Alexander Stadium, which will be the home for the 2022 Commonwealth Games. I became conscious that there were many young Blacks in sports, but I couldn't see or hear anything about any music or dance, so I made some enquiries. I should rewind for one second, because what was my interest in dance? In my village in Trinidad, I grew up with Shango [an African-Trinidadian religious practice], so I would hear those wonderful African drums and I would peek and look under the tent, and they were slitting throats of cocks and sheep and goats. I'm writing a book at the moment about the history of African and Caribbean dance in the UK, and I say that I was stained not by the blood of sacrifice, but by the drums of Africa. Those drums were so magnetic and powerful, and that stayed with me. It was always music … Trinidad implants in you this wonderful sense of carnival. Whether it's the way you study, the way you dance, the way you marry and bring children up, there's a sense of energy and colour and vibrancy that I could never wash away because *that is* Trinidad in me.

As I said, in Trinidad I was accustomed to going to the theatre and performing as well in my scout group. In London in the 1970s, I remember seeing Ekome dance company at what used to be the Commonwealth Institute in Kensington. That crystallised my links with what Shango was and what these beautiful people were doing on stage: powerful African and Caribbean dance. I laugh in the book when I say maybe I was drawn more to African dance because the company were about six people: one guy and five of the most beautiful women I've ever seen. My love for African dance was amplified through the Andersons – Barry and his sisters Lorna and Angela and others. They were so great. They were from Bristol, so this thing of dance was already in me, and then, when I went to Birmingham, I started to look around and saw there were no dance companies, there's no African drumming. I later heard of Hermin McIntosh, a young sister who had a small group called Sankofa. I contacted her, discussed what she was doing, and decided to explore dance with some of the young people who were on probation.

From the outset, I was determined that if I were to do something, it had to involve both 'clients' and 'non-clients'. I was still a Probation Officer on my 'probationary period'. Then I thought how, as a Probation Officer, can I impact people's lives, especially the youths who were on probation, without overtly attempting to be like God – you know? 'These are the lines, these are the laws of Moses, you break them and there's fire and brimstone.' We were getting a lot of that in the Black churches, we were getting a lot of that in schools, we were getting a lot of that from our parents, for whom, you know, everything was black and white. So the first thing I did in my office was get a lot of visual images – painting, artwork, sculptures – so Black and white could come and relate, so we'd have something to chat about, and I always had books, CDs and a little player. I wasn't a conventional Probation Officer. I had a little old Decca record player with calypso and reggae records. You don't go to your Probation Officer to listen to calypsos or for him to talk to you about books. They were like hashtags in my room – hashtags that you could tag along to!

I came to Birmingham in 1977, and by the end of 1977 I was not even a year in the Probation Service, but by then I was having clients and non-clients come into the probation office after working hours and we'd move the chairs around in the common room and the young people would practice 'drumming and dancing'! My colleagues said we were making too much noise, and that was certainly one way to lose a lot of probation friends!

Were they critical of what you were doing?

They were indeed. I was a young upstart, I was this, I was that, I'm telling officers we shouldn't have separate offices, but we should share offices and 'share clients' too! Then it got worse when the Service advertised a job for a community development worker and I said to my senior, 'I'm going after this job, this would really suit the way I want to work.' He said it was being advertised at a Senior Probation level, and as I've not even completed my probation, he would not agree. But I said, 'It's about community development, that's my thing, I love being out there, and we should be working within the community.' I asked if he would give me a reference because I'm going to apply. He said, 'No – in that case, you'd have to see the ACPO.' Basically, what he was saying to me – 'You're not even a fully fledged Probation Officer,' and I was saying, 'Hey, I'm 29, I bring with me at least some years of experience as a person living with and working within communities.' Nobody would give me a reference, but I thought, 'I'm going to apply,' I did, and I got the job!

That's when you realise who were your colleagues and who were not. Some said I got it because I was Black, I got it because I had a big mouth, I got it because of this, I got it because of that. We then had to find a building in the community, we bought two old houses side by side, on the corner of Wellington Road and Hamstead Road in Handsworth. Old buildings, we converted them to what I called The Handsworth Cultural Centre, deliberately avoiding any visible connection in the name with the Probation Service. And here is this Probation Officer talking to architects about – 'Okay, we need a dance studio here, this is going to be sprung wooden floors, this is going to be a photography room, this is a room I need sound-proofed because we're going to have a recording studio.' To me, it was quite simple: we cannot be talking about community development for the Probation Service and still be thinking of 'clients' and this and that. We need to think about community, and I'm going to be out there, let's create a space and call it the Handsworth Cultural Centre – that anyone could come into.

Some colleagues refused to speak to me after that. But some would come up to the centre and enjoy it and bring their 'clients'. They'd say, 'Let's go up to the Cultural Centre.' And we had a nice small café I had the garden landscaped by an English student, with thatched-roof seated areas, a sandpit with wooden sculptures, a sunken garden with tropical plants, and a lawned area where we hosted cultural events. There's a beautiful book by Kieran Connell called *Black Handsworth* [2019] in which he writes about the Handsworth Cultural Centre. I had some American professors who visited, who were shocked when they came to Handsworth and saw two houses knocked into one – they were, 'Is this where you do all this great work?!' They couldn't believe the number of people who were coming through there.

To me, I didn't realise it at the time, it was all about creative ways of working with so-called young people who were on the fringes, whether they had gone through the criminal justice system or they were liable at some point because they were young and Black. It was a different philosophy. I raised scholarships to send youths to Jamaica to study. I raised money and took a group of people to Ghana, to the University of Ghana, and we stayed there for six months doing arts and crafts and music, history and religion. We started up dance companies, one of the dance companies lasted for over 18 years in England, Kokuma dance theatre company, and members from Kokuma later established ACE Dance Company. It was about creating opportunities for others, and to this day that's where I am. I still volunteer with lots of groups, we do music online. Can you believe it? In my wonderful golden age of retirement, I started the Rupununi Music and Arts festival in Guyana, and we will celebrate our seventh anniversary in 2021!

Can I ask you one last thing? Can I ask you about your indentured heritage? I wondered if there's any sense you feel the legacies of your grandparents, your great-grandparents in what you've done? When I say that, I refer to your sense of community and of generosity.

It was my grandfather who came as an indentured labourer. At the end of the week, I believe, he'd get the same thing for his labours, a bag of rice or whatever. He would keep half and sell half. My grandfather became extremely wealthy. He had estates with cocoa, coffee, tonka beans – he used to mass-produce and sell. Granddad had something which he used to do every day – I don't do it every day but I wish I could – he ate the simplest food. My grandfather would be quite content with a roti, a cup of dahl and some aubergines or some baigan choka [roasted aubergine]. It's funny, my grandson, who's 21, makes his own roti and makes his own dahl puri [flatbread stuffed with split peas], something which I would never venture. Every time he comes to me, we will cook. My grandfather, if he could drink a cup of dahl every day, was the happiest man, and for many, many years in England I would have that!

For us growing up and because of the colonial system under which we were educated, there was the whole perception that India was this lost world where they came from, nobody was interested in India, we were interested in Trinidad, where we lived. My memory of my granddad is this simplicity of life, he never used to wear dhotis [a long loincloth resembling loose trousers], but he had dhotis. He was proud that he had educated his children, my dad and my auntie.

But the connection, when I reflect now, is that I'd like to make another trip to India. On my first trip, I went for spiritual reasons, I knew it was my source and I wanted to experience the energy of India. Even though my first experience I didn't feel anything, the second time I went back, I thought 'Yes.' I have often reflected I could go to one of those little villages around Cochin and settle there.

6

A Tribute to the Life of Rudy Narayan (1938–1998)

Lainy Malkani

People followed him because he was a courageous man.

(Sibghat Kadri QC)

I could not pinpoint the exact moment I heard the name Rudy Narayan, but his reputation as a champion fighter against injustice was well known, not just in London where he lived, but across many urban cities in England. In the late 1980s, at the height of Rudy's career, I was a young, aspirational journalist who was captivated by his passion to protect those who did not have the means to protect themselves. He was of my mother's generation, who had grown up in British Guiana and who travelled to the UK with a sense of hope and adventure only to find that racial injustice and inequality had seeped into every corner of life, threatening to crush the ambitions of so many people of colour – everyone except Rudy Narayan, a courageous lawyer who broke the rules to make the rules, who defended Black communities against a hostile police force and challenged the law profession to end racial discrimination in its ranks.

To fully appreciate the love and respect people have for this fearless civil rights barrister, you need to head to South London, stand back a little from the bustling Italian café on Brixton Road, and cast your eyes upwards. There you will find a Blue Plaque mounted on a red-brick Victorian building with the inscription: 'Barrister, Civil Rights Activist, Community Champion and Voice for the Voiceless'. It was here that Rudy practised law between 1987 and 1994. The windows, now draped with white net curtains, are a gateway to the past when Rudy set up a law centre that offered free legal advice to the community. He was known as a fearless barrister who was a thorn in the side of the establishment; lawmakers and the police alike. The former criminal and immigration barrister Sibghat Kadri QC, who first met Rudy as a student in 1969, a year after Rudy was called to the Bar, described him as 'a great cross-examiner', while leading human rights barrister Michael Mansfield QC went even further when he said that Rudy Narayan 'could have been the great Black barrister' of his generation.

The plaque has become one of the many treasures of Brixton, South London with its deep-rooted history of resistance to racial prejudice and injustice. During the 1980s and early 1990s the area earned its reputation as a place of oppression inflicted on the community by the police and the government. Acute deprivation and underinvestment created a fertile ground for community activism, and as a civil rights barrister, it was the law that Rudy Narayan used to challenge the establishment.

His office had an open door policy whereby members of the community, harassed by the police could go and air their grievances. More than that, it also became a refuge for the people of Brixton.

The former editor of *The Weekly Gleaner*, George Ruddock, described Rudy as an outstanding person and a big personality in the area. In 1995, as local people clashed with the police following the death of Wayne Douglas, George recalled how Rudy's office had become a makeshift newsroom:

Our offices were on Acre Lane, which was just down the road from where Rudy's offices were. So when *The Weekly Gleaner* was targeted in an arson attack, we had to get out. Rudy stepped in and offered his own premises as a way to ensure that our newspaper could be published. He put people's rights at the forefront, and was an advocate for equality and employment.

Rodney Hinds, now a journalist for *The Voice* newspaper, recalls meeting Rudy in 1982. At the time, he was working for *West Indian World*, one of the first newspapers aimed at an ethnic minority readership, owned by the publisher and newspaper proprietor Arif Ali. Hinds described Rudy as a powerful Black man in an elite profession: 'He was fearless and didn't suffer fools gladly.'

Born in 1938 in Essequibo, British Guiana, Rahasya Rudra Narayan was the ninth child of Sase Narayan, an Indian landowner, and his wife, Taijbertie. The family emigrated to the UK in 1953 when he was 15 years old. In his youth, he was employed in a variety of small jobs, including in one of the famous Lyons Tea Houses. In 1958, he went on to join the British Army, where he remained for seven years and rose to the rank of sergeant in the Royal Army Ordinance Corps. When he left in 1965, he had set his mind on a new career. He studied law at Lincoln's Inn, and was called to the Bar in 1968.

Sibghat Kadri QC was in his final year of study when Rudy graduated, and remembers a more conservative man in those early days:

Rudy came from Guyana, a former British colony, and he joined the British Army, so he believed in the great Motherland. He trusted the Empire very much and he thought like the establishment. Within a year, he realised that he trusted the British Empire too much, the so-called British flag, its freedoms and citizens were for white people, not him.

The late 1960s was a time when racial tensions were mounting. The damning effect of Enoch Powell's infamous Rivers of Blood speech, delivered in the same year that Rudy graduated, laid bare

Britain's divided nation. Like paint peeling off a whitewashed wall to reveal hidden layers of decay, the allure of the Motherland was beginning to fade.

It was a rude awakening, even for Sibghat Kadri QC: 'It was unimaginable that the legal profession might be institutionally racist, [but in] those days we had very different judges. They were all trained during the Empire, and they didn't think Black or Asians were any good.'

It was from this moment Sibghat Kadri QC says that Rudy became a leading fighter against institutional racism in the legal profession and the police. In 1969, together they set up the Association of Afro, Asian and Caribbean Lawyers, which later became the Society of Black Lawyers (SBL).

Raissa Aude Uwineza, National Co-Vice Chair of the SBL, in a speech reported on the *Society of Black Lawyers* website, praised their vision and leadership at the unveiling of Rudy's Blue Plaque in 2010. He explained that the two men were accused by the Chairman of the Bar Council at the time of acting divisively and against the traditions of the Bar. They even faced accusations of creating a form of 'legal Apartheid'. Uwineza said:

> The irony of his comments is that prior to 1973, only UK citizens could become solicitors, and therefore, by excluding ethnic minority lawyers on the basis of this citizenship test, the legal profession had itself been operating a form of apartheid for hundreds of years.

As a civil rights lawyer, Rudy's name quickly became associated with an uncompromising and determined fight for racial justice. He passionately defended those who were victimised, who were considered to be the underdogs of society and the poor.

The 1980s were difficult years for Black communities all over the country. He achieved successes in defending those accused of rioting in Bristol, Handsworth and Brixton. In a career spanning over 26 years, he had developed a reputation as a formidable defence barrister who had lived through some of the toughest periods in the history of race relations in the UK. In the aftermath of the Brixton Riots in 1981, Rudy set up the Brixton Defence Committee to defend many of those who had been arrested and thrown in jail. In an interview with LBC radio that same year, he told a reporter that the motive of the Defence Committee was to raise financial support to defend those whom he was convinced were innocent and to provide 'political and moral support' to their families. He was unflinching in his dedication to root out racism in the police. He said there was an urgent need to improve police race relations and for more Black judges.

In that same year, he also demanded justice for the grieving families of the New Cross fire, whose sons and daughters had been the victims of a brutal racial attack in which 13 young people died.

He was equally acerbic towards the legal profession in court, highlighting at every opportunity institutional racism as he saw it. He faced his first disciplinary hearing in Birmingham when he called solicitors, barristers and judges racist after discovering that prisoners who requested his representation had been told they should have a white barrister. In 1980 he was reprimanded for being rude to a judge, and in 1982 he claimed that the Attorney General and Director of Public Prosecutions were in collusion with the National Front. These clashes with the legal profession eventually ended his career, and in 1994 he was disbarred for professional misconduct.

Rudy died on Sunday 28 June 1998 of cirrhosis of the liver. I am told that his funeral, held at St Matthew's Church in Brixton, was packed to the rafters by mourners who felt the need to honour his memory. Knowing as I do what a Guyanese funeral is like, I imagine the service was a vibrant one despite the sadness of the occasion.

His memory does live on. In this, the 40th anniversary of the Brixton uprisings, he will be remembered just as he was in 2018 when the community gathered at Lambeth Town Hall in Brixton to commemorate his life. Arthur Torrington, Director of the Windrush Foundation, invited me, as we had often spoken about my fascination with this outspoken and fiery barrister.

The eclectic mix of people who took their seats at the commemoration felt it too. It was an impressive gathering, from prominent radio and television presenters and actors to musicians and community activists, Rudy's memory had united them all, and they had inspirational stories to tell. We met on an unusually warm evening, and the doors were wedged open to let a gentle breeze saunter in from the streets and cool a captivated audience. I think that was the way the eminent barrister and firebrand would have liked it. He was a man of the people with an open door policy for those in most need: Black, brown, white working-class.

Alex Pascall, who was one of the first Black radio presenters on BBC Radio London, recalled the many times Rudy was interviewed on his programme *Black Londoners*. He was also the Chair of the Black Londoners Advisory Committee, a responsibility he took seriously when time allowed. The flautist Keith Waithe's cool and evocative sounds reminded us of Rudy's Indian-Guyanese roots, while his daughter Yasmeen spoke of the pride she had for her father, who had given so much to the community. The Dub poet Linton Kwesi Johnson, a former member of the Black Panthers, recited 'Tings and Times', and set the scene of Brixton in the 1980s, which was one of deprivation and police harassment. Before he began, he was reminded of the time Rudy had offered his services should members of the Black Panther movement require it. His words were met with a round of applause that rang through the town hall.

Many of those who had gathered to commemorate the life of Rudy had spoken of how they had been captivated by this larger-than-life figure. In Brixton, he stood out from the crowd with his thick, curly black hair, long sideburns and dark glasses. He spoke the Queen's English in a determined and unflinchingly confident style that I am told intimidated his opposite numbers in court.

One of the stories that captivated me at the commemoration was from the reggae musician and producer Dennis Bovell. In a pre-recorded interview projected on the wall above the stage, he told us how he had been arrested by the police, tried and convicted for his alleged part in a fracas that had broken out at a sound system clash in 1974. Dennis was represented by Rudy at appeal, and the case was thrown out. It was an emotional recognition of Rudy's ability to persist when all else seemed hopeless, and a reminder that were it not for Rudy's interventions, so many lives could have taken a very different turn. Dennis echoed the sentiments so eloquently written on the wall at 413 Brixton Road. Rudy was a 'champion of the people', he said, with 'a fearless defence of minority people'.

I struggle to imagine how Rudy would have felt about these accolades. It is my sense that he was a man consumed with an inner sense of duty to protect the people. It came naturally to him. But his constant struggle to change the law from within was a different battle entirely, and one which in the end cost him his career. He wanted to see changes to the legal profession that would root out racism and create a level playing field for all people. He was conscious, too, of the need to provide a support mechanism for young Black and brown lawyers of the future. He did not fail. The Afro, Asian and Caribbean Lawyers Association he set up along with his friend and colleague Sibghat Kadri QC, now known as the Society of Black Lawyers, still flourishes to this day. His constant complaining and relentless exposure of racism eventually led to the Bar Council's first race relations committee in 1984, and changes to the Race Relations Act that would prohibit race discrimination in the legal profession – a legacy that has never been forgotten.

Rudy was also a prolific writer. He published several books, including *Barrister for the Defence: Trial by Jury and How to Survive It!* In it, he observes that the Bar was dominated by those who were male, white and middle-class. He also called on his profession to become more democratic, while urging the public to become more aware. It is a powerfully written book, and reading it now, in the twenty-first century, it is clear that he was ahead of his time. The issues he raised more than three decades ago are still prevalent today.

As a writer, he excelled, but he had other literary talents too: as a script writer. It fell upon the actor and friend to Rudy, Rudolph Walker, to reveal the story behind the eight-part series for BBC television called *Black Silk*. Rudolph, with a warm smile on his face, recalled how Rudy had thrust the script in his hands with a simple request to get the series commissioned. *Black Silk* was based on Rudy's own life experiences at the Bar, and in November 1985 the first episode was broadcast on national television. It was called 'A Long Way Away'. Rudolph Walker played the starring role of Larry Scott, the only Black barrister working in a London law firm. The magnitude of this achievement should not be underestimated. Not only had Rudy found a way to take his campaign work to a new level, but he used mass media as his platform to reveal the struggles of people on the margins of society. Larry Scott was based on the life of Rudy Narayan, a Caribbean barrister of Indian descent. It was a milestone in broadcasting history, and nothing like it has ever happened again since.

Of course, while there were immense victories and highlights in Rudy's career, there were also extreme lows. He was highly critical of the profession he loved, calling out racism and those with racist views when he encountered them. It had a huge detrimental effect on his career. Had he not been so outspoken, had he couched his words in politer legalese, then perhaps he would not have been disciplined by the Bar Council in 1974 or again in 1980, when he was reprimanded for being rude to a judge. But that would not have been Rudy.

Nevertheless, his legacy remains untarnished for the people he served. At the commemoration, many of the people who were present remembered the days when the British Black community felt under siege. They were not bystanders in the fight for equality and justice in the area, but stood side by side with Rudy in order to achieve it. Now they brought their children and grandchildren to hear stories of how one man joined forces to defend and protect them.

Judging by the warmth and depth of feeling expressed at his commemoration, I am sure his legacy will continue to have an impact. I am grateful to Arthur Torrington for my invite. It was a special evening of remembrance, but I can't help wondering what he would have made of today's challenges in the fight against racial injustice and oppression. What would he have made of race relations in twenty-first-century London, with the Black Lives Matter campaign gathering strength and the misery of those who lost their lives in the Grenfell fire?

I suspect he would not have let the events of the last two decades fill him with despair, but rather the opposite – after all, he was a champion of the poor, and there is still so much work to be done.

ACKNOWLEDGEMENTS

With thanks to Sigbhat Kadri QC, George Ruddock, Rodney Hinds, Rudolph Walker and Arthur Torrington for your memories of Rudy Narayan.

BIBLIOGRAPHY

'Civil Rights: Rudy Narayan Honoured', *Operation Black Vote*, 15 November 2010, www.obv.org.uk/news-blogs/civil-rights-rudy-narayan-honoured, accessed 31 January 2021.

Narayan, R., *Barrister for the Defence: Trial by Jury and How to Survive It!* (London: Justice Books, 1985).

'Rudy Narayan', *Wikipedia*, https://en.wikipedia.org/wiki/Rudy_Narayan, accessed 31 January 2021.

Uwineza, R.A., 'Remembering Rudy Narayan: Blue Heritage Plaque for SBL Co-founder', *Society of Black Lawyers*, https://societyof blacklawyers.co.uk/remembering-rudy-narayan-blue-heritage-plaque-for-sbl-co-founder/, accessed 31 January 2021.

7

Pepperpot

Gordon Warnecke

My agent has sent me to audition for a role in *EastEnders*. An arranged marriage is the plot line (there's a surprise), and it's only six episodes. I'm sitting in the foyer waiting to go in. I look up at a screen and watch Julia Smith, the producer of *EastEnders*, talking about the imminent ten-year anniversary of the show. I was never a fan of *EastEnders*, and working in the sterile environment of a TV studio for a few weeks on something I don't care for is giving me huge reservations about going through with the audition. 'Balls to this,' I'm thinking. I stand up, ready to walk out of the door and go home, when someone calls me in for the audition.

We exchange pleasantries, and this is followed by a half-hearted reading by me for the part I'm up for. I'm asked what my heritage is. When I started out in the business, I lied about where my parents came from, as I was often only seen for Asian parts. I kept quiet about my dad being a white German and told a lie about my mother coming from India. But for the past couple of years I have decided to tell the truth. 'I was born in Highgate, North London. My father comes from Germany and my mother comes from Guyana in South America … her grandparents came from Northern India.' This is met by furrowed brows and an awkward silence from the three jolly white BBC people auditioning me. There is a long pause.

Then one of them says, 'But you do have Asian friends, don't you?'

12 AUGUST 1873, CALCUTTA: MY GREAT-GRANDFATHER LEAVES INDIA FOR GUYANA, EMIGRANT PASS 4103

My great-grandfather, Mungal Singh, came from Awoa (now Awaon), a village near Azamgarh, Uttar Pradesh, in the far north of India. His caste designation was Chuttree, and he was from a high, or warrior, caste. His family were probably landowners or rulers. During the nineteenth century, Uttar Pradesh had seen a lot of political unrest, and this may have been why my great-grandfather chose to leave India: a chance for other opportunities and a better life.

Mungal Singh sailed, without his family, from Calcutta to Berbice, British Guiana, on the ship *Sussex*. My great-grandfather was probably considered a big man with a commanding presence because, as the ship's log shows, he was given the role of sirdar on the boat. This meant that he was put in charge of 25 fellow emigrants. Once he had arrived in Guyana, he worked on a sugar plantation in Port Mourant, Berbice, where again he was made a sirdar. Sirdars could be respected, but they were also often feared and hated. They were the buffer between the white overseers and the canecutters and weeders on the plantation. My great-grandfather would have benefited from having access to the overseers' world, and he would have learnt English.

12 FEBRUARY 1872, CALCUTTA: MY GREAT-GRANDMOTHER LEAVES INDIA FOR BRITISH GUIANA, EMIGRANT PASS 453

At the age of nine, my great-grandmother-to-be, Leelmoney, left her village, Sutia, with her family. Sutia was in Poonooleah, a district in Northern India. They departed from Calcutta on the boat *Poonah* a year before my great-grandfather, her future husband, left India. On arrival, her family were sent to work on a sugar plantation in Smythfields, close to Port Mourant. After their indenture, they stayed and opened a grocery store. When my great-grandfather's indenture was over, he purchased land, prospered and eventually met Leelmoney. Mungal and Leelmoney had six children, and all had Christian and Indian names. It was Mungal's decision to have his children marry in a Christian church so they all became converts, meaning that they would be 'above' the other villagers. This may explain my mother's attitude when she lived in England.

8 MAY 1923, LETTER KENNY, GUYANA: MY MOTHER IS BORN

When I started out in the business, I lied about where my parents came from. I was often only seen for Asian parts, so I kept quiet about my dad being a white German and said that my mother came from India. At the time, I felt no guilt about distorting the facts; I was young and eager to get the work, and physically I knew I fitted the bill. Only later on did I realise that what I could bring to a part, irrespective of what my (true) nationality was, was more important.

My mother, Iris, was raised in Letter Kenny, Berbice, British Guiana by her parents, Angelina Mangal Singh and Thomas Brian Budhoo. The house she grew up in was like a long, white box with a series of lattice shutters. It was built on slender wooden stilts, as the local area was prone to flooding. It was bought by my great-grandfather and given to my grandfather as a dowry when he gave Angelina away.

Iris was the youngest of eight children. She and her brother Walter, the second youngest, were doted upon by their older siblings, who became their surrogate parents when Angelina and

Thomas died in the children's early teens. Life became hard for the family, unemployment in the villages was high, and Iris's chances of marrying a suitable young man and starting a family, something expected of her at the time, were very slim. The siblings had all been to school and were very involved in the Christian church. As they lived among Hindu and Muslim farmers, there were few suitors for the Budhoos. Also, the custom of having an adequate dowry hampered the Budhoos' attempts to make suitable matches.

My mother worked as a secretary for a small accounting firm in Berbice. She saved her earnings while her elder sisters, very involved with the church, kept the house running and remained watchful over Iris. One of her brothers was Director of the Rice Producers Association. Another brother drank heavily and gambled a lot. He died in his late fifties, having literally drunk himself to death. As with many women in Guyana at that time, her life was very restricted. Most of her friends either moved to Georgetown or went overseas to live with relatives. Both my mother and her youngest brother Walter had plans to fly the nest, and Walter was the first to do so, leaving for America in 1948 to study Mathematics at Howard University.[1]

My mother was in her late twenties when she left to start a new life England in 1954. Together with her savings, money from her brother Walter in America meant that she was able to fly to England with her close friend Annie. It must have been a big step for Iris and Walter to leave such a close-knit family, but they all wished her the best, knowing that both she and Walter had been desperate to 'get out'.

---

[1] Walter left for America on a scholarship to Howard University in Washington, DC, having completed his Overseas Cambridge exams early. The university was known as a Black university and recruited students from the West Indies. He first studied International Relations and joined the India Club, where he met Indians from India, which led him to work for the Indian Consulate while he pursued his graduate degree in Economics at New York University, where he met his wife Shirley. He did not think that he would become a maths teacher, but he had a 'flair for maths' and became a high school maths teacher in New York.

On arrival in London, Iris and Annie shared a small bedsit. I remember my mother telling me how cold and different it was from the warmth of Guyana. Annie eventually moved on, and my mother stuck it out in the cold damp bedsit, working for a few months in a factory before getting a secretarial job for an accounting firm in London.[2] She was teased by the other girls in the office, as her boss, Mr Edward Warnecke (Ted), had taken an obvious shine to her. Ted summoned the courage to ask the new secretary out for dinner at a Chinese restaurant; she agreed, and by their third date, he had proposed to her.

Ted and Iris married in 1961, and lived in Highgate before buying a modest three-bedroom house in the London suburb of Greenford. They had two boys, myself and my brother Colin, who died tragically in a car accident when he was 18. Up until that moment, life had been sweet, growing up with loving parents in the suburbs. The loss remained with my parents until the end of their lives, and has stayed with me throughout mine.

During the 1960s and 1970s, Greenford was predominantly white, with Asian families moving in gradually during the early 1980s. I was one of the very few dark-skinned children in my infant and junior schools. I fondly remember those long, hot summers growing up in Greenford, playing football in the park with my friends until it was too dark to see the ball, holidays at Butlin's and the many parties my parents and their friends had. I remember the small group of multi-cultural friends they were closest to, and each weekend, they would take it in turns to hold parties at each other's houses. Esther and Inger were German, and were married to Frank and Clive respectively, who were both from Trinidad. Skavoola was Greek, and her husband, Joel, was Chinese-Trinidadian.

---

2   Annie Kennard became a doctor and married a doctor. They raised a family and lived in North West London. My mother kept in contact with her sporadically over the years, and I remember visiting them as a child.

Figure 7.1 Mum, Dad and me, 1962, before
we moved from Highgate to Greenford.
(Photo courtesy of Gordon Warnecke)

When I was growing up, my mother generally cooked English
food. This was because when she lived in Guyana, her older sisters
did all the cooking. I can still hear the men's heavy West Indian
accents in the kitchen as they helped to cook a Guyanese curry.
The food was washed down with Watneys pale ale from a small
keg and Dubonnet, and of course a lot of rum. Clive would also
often cook fried garlic pork (at least eight large bulbs of the garlic
would have been marinating in a jar of white wine vinegar for
weeks). There was always dancing and music. Vinyl records played
on the hi-fi system (with Dolby noise reduction for cassettes!),

invariably calypso records along with *Hits of the 70s*, spun on the turntable while I would secretly sit at the top of the stairs in my pyjamas, peeking through the banister rails watching the grown-ups dancing. I was often spotted and told to come and join in with the dancing.

Despite the mix of nationalities, my mother always considered herself 'an English woman' and had a slight disdain for the Asian families who moved in to the area later on in the 1980s. I always suspected this was rooted in the way she was brought up in colonial Guyana – her Christian upbringing and the fact that she didn't come from a farming background, made her feel above the other Indians in Letter Kenny.

Sometimes Guyanese relations would come and visit us. My father would get exasperated when these relatives would turn up two or three hours late, usually without apologising, but he had to remember the latecomers went by GMT (Guyanese Mean Time). He never got used to their timekeeping, especially as he was German and, of course, he was always punctual. Some of the relatives who visited were from the Luckhoo family. My grandmother's other sister had married Edward Luckhoo, who was the last Governor General of Guyana and who also became the Acting President when Guyana became a republic on 23 February 1970. Every time the visiting Guyanese relatives and friends had left our house, I noticed my mother adopted a thicker Guyanese accent. Once, I remember she said to me 'Pass the rice, boy.' I commented that I was 'Gordon' or 'son', not 'boy', and that she had spent too long listening to how our relatives spoke. She calmly replied, 'What are you talking about? Now, pass me the Rice Boy.' My mistake. Rice Boy was the name on the box of a plug-in rice steamer that sat on top of a cupboard in the kitchen!

Walter, my mother's brother in America, married Shirley, a Russian Jewish woman from New York. They had two children, Philip and Marina, with whom I remain close to this day. Every year they would come to England and spend the summer with us.

It was a cultural awakening when the Americans arrived, as they appeared to have everything, even colour televisions! I remember that my aunt bought us a large, white fridge, as she deemed our 'little English fridge' far too small.

My father was a socialist, but never said aloud what he thought about our American family's excessiveness. Over the years, I witnessed his disillusionment with his socialist principles, and this was sad to see. In the Second World War, he had served in the British Army in North Africa, working with the Royal Engineers. In the early 1950s, he was called up again, but due to his socialist beliefs, he became a Conscientious Objector. I still have the letter he typed to the Home Office explaining his reasons for not wanting to fight in another war. After this, he was not called up to fight again.[3] He became the Secretary for the West London branch for the Socialist Party of Great Britain. I would sometimes accompany him to the meetings they held in Red Lion Square. How could he, working as an accountant, try and live by his socialist principles while consumerism was all around him. When I was a teenager and my political ideas were beginning to form, my father and I had many heated discussions over Sunday lunch. These were usually about why I did not think socialism could work in the West. My mother would often call a halt to our arguments, and we would dutifully finish our roast dinner in silence and then continue our argument in the kitchen, out of

_____

3   My father's dad was born in Germany, and worked for a German count (Alexander Münster, the son of Prince George Herbert of Münster). The Count owned Maresfield Park in Sussex, and would visit it frequently. It was here that my grandfather met my grandmother, who came from Devon and worked there as a cook. At the outbreak of the First World War, the Count and my grandfather were interned on the Isle of Wight. After they were released at the end of the war, my grandfather and his wife had three children and went back to Germany to carry on working for the Count at his castle in Münster (now called Schloss Derneburg). My dad was born in Derneburg in 1921. After the principalities in Germany were broken up, the family continued to live in Germany for a few years before moving back to England in 1929, when my dad was eight years old. They settled in Lewes in Sussex, and he and his father became naturalised as British citizens on 20 April 1936.

her earshot and over the washing up. As much as my Christian mother loved her atheist husband, she had no time for his politics (or mine) at the dinner table. She was quite content to be in England, having come from Guyana, where she and her family had very little compared to what she had now. Our trip to Guyana in 1974 reinforced this.

My parents took my brother Colin and I to Guyana for a family holiday when I was 11 and he was seven. My memories of this holiday are still incredibly vivid. I can recall the good times we had there, the relatives we visited, the food we ate. I remember seeing the sugar cane, which was growing in shiny rows, and passing sugar refineries in the car. We picnicked on 63 Beach, a beautiful, deserted sandy beach in Berbice. The sea lapped at our feet while we were shown how to splice a coconut with a cutlass. We stayed mainly in New Amsterdam with my mum's closest sister, Eileen, who was now a missionary for the church. We also stayed at the family house for a few days. My mother's brothers and sisters showed us the same wonderful hospitality we encountered everywhere in Guyana. Much to my father's annoyance and disbelief, the women never sat with us to eat even though they had made a feast of food. It was the Guyanese way. I can remember sitting for hours in a rocking chair on the porch of the wooden stilted house, blissfully enjoying guineps (a fruit similar to a lychee) and listening to the sound the stones made as they dropped into a wooden basket at my feet.

Many years later, my cousin, Marina Budhos, who is a writer, recorded a conversation with my mother.[4] Marina has done a lot of research into our family's history and written a number of books. My mother told Marina that she had hated going back to Guyana. She had already been back twice before our family holiday, and although she loved her family very much, her new roots in England had taken hold.

---

4   The author wishes to express his heartfelt thanks to his cousin, Marina Budhos, whose research has been invaluable to him.

'My husband loved it,' she told Marina. 'He liked the sand and the sun and the sea. The people were so generous, lots of invitations. Ted cried when he left. I didn't want to stay. I hated it. Ted would take the boys out for a walk late morning. It was so hot, I would have to lie down. Mad dogs and Englishmen ... I used to tell him to keep them in the cool. My sister could not believe Ted was putting clothes out on the washing line. "Look at that white man putting out those clothes," my sister said.'

My father passed away on 21 January 2000, the date of my brother's birthday. My mother, Iris, survived him by ten years. Recently, my son Daniel has begun to show great interest in his roots. He is very keen to go to Guyana, and like me, he loves Caribbean food. The other day, he asked me to FaceTime him so I could show him how to make jerk chicken for a barbecue he was having. He still relies on his old man's jerk paste to take home with him when he comes around to visit me. My cousin Marina and I have recently discovered, through DNA tracing, many second cousins in America. Thanks to Marina's desire to find out more about our roots, I agreed to join the DNA tracing agency after years of only connecting with my immediate cousins in the States. I was very surprised to see we have so many second cousins in America, all of whom are very close to each other. Having met some of them last year, I feel more aware of my identity and more grounded by this awareness. I have a sense of belonging to a bigger 'family' than I originally thought I had.

Daniel and I met my second cousins for the first time last year. They seem to be keeping the Guyanese way of life going, and thankfully, because of our interest in Guyanese food, they share their recipes with me. When we FaceTime each other, their Guyanese accents are still strong despite having lived in America for many years. The older I get, the more I seem to be drawn to Guyana, and this has been augmented by my son's desire to find out more about his roots. My mother wanted to become more English when she lived here, yet I question my own identity on a daily basis. Yes, I'm a North London boy who has always felt English, but I am being challenged internally on a daily basis by what is going on around me politically and by my own (late) recognition of my heritage. The Windrush scandal and the Black Lives Matter movement have raised, among many other important issues, a re-examination of our past and encouraged (British) people to look at their own history and consider how colonialism has played a big part in how this country has been shaped.

8

Scratching the Surface: A Speculative Feminist Visual History of other Windrush Itineraries

Tao Leigh Goffe

hysteria
1. *Medicine*. Originally: a (supposed) physical disorder of women attributed to displacement or dysfunction of the uterus, and characterized particularly by a sensation of fullness in the abdomen and chest, with choking or breathlessness

(Oxford English Dictionary)

Family history is colonial history. How, then, to understand the vernacular photographic record and what is missing about the Windrush era, itself already an omission from British history? Since the inception of the technology of photography in the 1840s, the family photo album as an heirloom to be passed down, vertically, has formed the flesh of blood relation. The family album is also a literary surface inscribed with multiple meanings about race, gender, sexuality, class and who does not belong in the family tree. The visuality of collected images forms the fleshy proof of a seemingly biological argument for bourgeois belonging and familial intimacy. Blood is proof of kinship; the family portrait is flesh, and often colonial belonging.

Because family history is inevitably colonial history, I am invested in what and who is left out of the family album and outside of colonial history. Of particular (and selfish) interest to me is the impossibility of subjects of African and Chinese heritage. Photographs of Afro-Chinese families pose a challenge to the British colonial Trinidad experiment that wished to introduce Chinese labour to the Caribbean plantation to replace Africans in the early nineteenth century. The 'experiment' documented in a secret Parliamentary Papers memorandum predicted the races would not mix. African and Asian people did, of course, 'mix'; and many subsequent channels of migration were formed from Africa meeting Asia (both China and India) in the Caribbean. Where do we see these descendants present in the routes of the Windrush generation?

Distancing myself from the binary of either a symptomatic or surface reading, I am invested in undoing the logic and violence of the colonial plantation, which is a logic of racial enclosure. How do photographs bear witness to my subjectivity as a British woman of African and Asian heritage who lives in the United States? It may not be intuitive, but the family album is a structure of racial enclosure too. Ordered by the fictions of race and policing of class and colour, the sentimentality of the family album makes it seem innocent or objective. Its potential, though, for violence is epistemic in the knowledge it produces. And so, against the scripts of colonial nostalgia, I am most interested in the images that live as *orphans* beyond the family album. Taken as a visual argument and against the burden of proof of genealogy, I scratch the surface of colonial-era photography to grapple with how the stories told of another Windrush, of Afro-Chinese womanhood and other women of colour who are in conflict with the colonial historiography of the Americas. These routes bring me to the metropole London, the place of my birth, and where other women I will discuss have lived.

The forgetting of Afro-Chinese histories, and furthermore of Afro-Chinese women, is an example of what it means to be beyond the interest or comprehension of coloniality. I look to forgotten women, scratched out of history and the family tree, and the process of forgetting in the visual work of artists Albert Chong and Richard Fung. Their investigations interlace with my own queries into family albums and tracing my own story of Black Pacific and Chinese Atlantic crossings, being myself a migrant from the United Kingdom to the United States. Though I am a 'new immigrant' to the Western hemisphere, I have been here before, many times over. As an Afro-Chinese person, as a Black person, I am not afforded the immigrant's amnesia to forget the violent institutions of racial slavery and racial indenture in whose wake people of African, Chinese and Indian descent live.

The plantation and suffering do not, of course, define the entirety of our lives, and yet the violent affective structure does define history. The plantation is a limit that determines why the photographs are missing for so many families, colonial subjects. The epistemic violence of erasing the histories of people of colour, a European colonial tactic, deliberately erased African and Asian people's histories on those continents in order to more easily subjugate them. If we are lucky, we have a few scattered photographs that provide a visual clue to not only the faces of our ancestors, but potentially a more intimate understanding of the quotidian lives of our forebears. If not, we must hazard to engage, to imagine, in the conditional tense of possibility and speculation, about the centuries before and unnamed ancestors.

My mother encountered a set of photographs in Miami in April 2017 that raised many such questions for us. Her cousin, who she had then recently become reacquainted with after decades and formed a telephone friendship with, named Chris, emailed my mother scans of the archive of photographs of his aunts (her aunts). He had been the guardian of these pictures, in excess of an album, for many decades. My mother had never met this side of the family. Her father would not, or could not, speak of them or his mother. A bachelor without children of his own, Chris bestowed the archive of his Aunt Hyacinth to us, his cousins, whom he barely knew.

It is an inevitable fact that we are all descended from generations and generations of 'hysteric' women, diagnosed or not. By 'hysteric', I mean wandering, drawing from the dictionary definition and epigraph of this essay, women with displaced and dysfunctional uteruses who refused to conform to patriarchal norms, whether by choice or biology. I don't know her, Hyacinth Lee, but she was one of these women. This essay is an attempt to reckon with genealogies of hysteric women through family photography and the limits to what we can ever know for sure when someone has been scratched out of the family tree. I attempt to imagine Afro-Chinese women who were part of the shadow archive of the voyage of the *Windrush* from Jamaica to the UK. My maternal grandfather did not know her either, his sister, Hyacinth. She, like so many optimistic West Indians, was part of an emergent class of labourers who migrated to the United Kingdom in the 1950s from Jamaica. Crossing the Atlantic, they became racialised as Black, whether they had been in the Caribbean or not.

My maternal grandfather made other transatlantic and transpacific journeys of racial formation from Hong Kong, where he grew up, to Jamaica, where he was born, to the United States, where he died. My research has so far been an attempt to illuminate the invisible circuitry of Black and Asian life beyond colonial circuits. I trace the lives of subjects across the British Empire by retracing Pacific and Atlantic Afro-Asian itineraries. So, I follow my grandfather and his siblings, of so-called 'half relation', born to Black mothers and Chinese fathers in Jamaica, to tell a full story of errantry.

The Chinese Atlantic is defined by the channels of what I describe as the institution of 'racial indenture', of the British transporting indentured Chinese and East Indian labourers to replace enslaved Africans on West Indian plantations.[1] Subsequent to the failure of Chinese indentureship in Jamaica, a Chinese merchant and shopkeeper class from the same home villages in South China as the indentured labourers, travelled voluntarily to the Caribbean seeking entrepreneurial opportunity. These ventures were intended to be short-term, return trips, but investments were made and children were born, often to local women, Black women. The discontinuity between the first wave of forced labour of indenture and the free merchant class that followed is an archival break, a gap, that has not been accounted for. In both waves, it was mostly men who migrated, whether indentured labourers or merchants, they usually ended up staying in the Caribbean and fathering children. Edwin, my grandfather, and Hyacinth, his sister, were siblings, the result of these Afro-Chinese conjugal intimacies, living parallel lives across continents, born to Black mothers and Chinese fathers in Kingston, Jamaica.

I do not call the siblings 'half' in relation because of the arith metic of identity, of racial and genealogical fractions, performing a narrative of a biological essentialism I am not invested in. My mother did not know her Aunt Hyacinth, nor did she know her father's mother – an Afro-Jamaican woman we believed for decades was Indo-Jamaican because it was what we had been told. Her name was Irene Caldwell, and as far as I know, my grandfather did not interact with his mother Irene upon his return to Jamaica in 1952, though she did not live far away from his home in Kingston, and he knew this. He had spent his life being raised by another mother, his Chinese stepmother, in Hong Kong's New Territories during the Second Sino-Japanese War and Second World War. When my grandfather was alive, he would not, or perhaps could not, answer questions about that life of a Black

1   Tao Leigh Goffe, 'Guano in Their Destiny: Race, Geology, and a Philosophy of Indenture', *Amerasia Journal*, 45:1 (2019), pp. 27–49.

boyhood spent in China. So I have been tracing his Black Pacific itinerary since his death.

The surfaces of Hyacinth's photographs are literally scratched up. It is hard to tell if faces are scratched out or highlighted as if an honorific halo. The history of the Chinese in the Caribbean has been muted and is also one of mutilation. Flesh was mutilated by the whip, by the overseer, during racial indenture. While there is no photographic record, or visual evidence, we know this because of depositions of protest from the 1870s in Cuba. Many Chinese across the Caribbean became fugitive and breached their indenture contracts, deserting plantations. The photographic emulsion, the light-sensitive colloid, comes in touch with a surface that then provides a burden of representation and racial proof. How, then, to join the discontinuity of multiple points of inflection in colonial history: Chinese indenture, Chinese merchant arrival to the Caribbean, and the *Windrush*? The photographs Chris gave us are a record of mid-century life that answered questions by showing us a life not often seen, of a Black woman in 1950s London.

Scratched, some faces are obscured. They appear almost colour-corrected or hand-tinted in a do-it-yourself fashion, with some faces being highlighted or coloured in, in red, yellow, green or blue. I do not know who did this to the photographs. Maybe it was Hyacinth when she looked back at these images depicting her British life. I only have scans of the photographs. So I draw what textural information I can from the materiality of the digital on computer screens. This is women's history, scratched out, the 'irresponsible reproducers', as sociologist Dorothy Roberts poignantly described how the state imagined working Black women as a problem in late colonial Jamaica.

Hyacinth is much like the witchy women Silvia Frederici writes of, the reproductive source of labour-power, purposely erased from history because of a threat to the patriarchal capitalist order. Women, the means of production, are concealed. Mental illness is concealed. My mother knew not to ask further when her father said he had two *foofool* sisters, literally and derisively 'idiots', a catch-all for mental illness. Was this hereditary? What of the other sister? Was her name Lucille? It was believed that Hyacinth died in the UK, and though she had a home, she appeared to be homeless. Word was sent to her mother in Jamaica about her mental decline.

To periodise Hyacinth as entirely of the Windrush generation would be to slate her for the lazy casting of a Netflix period piece on postwar Britain. The *Empire Windrush*, her majesty's transport, a vessel beckoned by the British Nationality Act of 1948, all at once defines the historical presence of Caribbean people in England and also forms other elisions and silences regarding race. The very question of the 'Other Windrush' is a question of who is pictured as being or looking Caribbean. I heard Hyacinth was heartbroken. Perhaps she was like Stuart Hall's heartbroken sister whom he writes of in his memoir. Hall's sister faced electric shock treatment after a breakdown, having been barred from being in a romantic relationship with a darker-skinned Black man. Unwed too, did Hyacinth perhaps suffer such a heartbreak? Or perhaps it was the heartbreak that many colonial subjects who go to the metropole face, of colourism and racism, alienated as a Black woman in a foreign white land? But maybe Hyacinth became Black in England like Stuart Hall did. Like him, maybe she was brown in Jamaica, designating a non-Black identity of middle-class status.

Caribbean is not a race, and yet, as a demonym, it comes with many assumptions, especially from non-West Indians. Caribbean denotes an Indigeneity that is often ignored; it performs its own set of erasures and elisions. Amerindian people who still exist across the Caribbean are often casually erased as though a relic of the past. While the recognition in British history of the significance of the *Empire Windrush* is important to add to the colonial timeline, it is also just that, a pivotal point on a timeline of multiculturalist myth-making. The fraught relationship between

British nationalism and Caribbean subjecthood cannot be encapsulated by one voyage because there were many other Windrushes, before and after 1948. Other ships and timelines of colonial subjecthood and metropole homegoings of disobedient children, such as Hannah Lowe's *Ormonde* (London: Hercules Editions, 2014), tell these stories: in Lowe's case, the story of her Afro-Chinese Jamaican father's arrival to the UK in 1947. Following the *Ormonde*, Lowe notes the arrival of the *Almanzora* the following year, also before the *Windrush*. Hazel Carby has written of her Afro-Jamaican father's posting in the Royal Air Force before the *Windrush* in *Imperial Intimacies* (London: Verso, 2019). Many ships docked after 1948; are they any less important?

My father's parents arrived on different ships sailing from Jamaica to London in 1954 and 1955, and met in the UK. The many itineraries of Black, Chinese and Indian subjectivity across time and space challenge convenient colonial timelines. I grew up in London and migrated to New York as a child, and my father gave me the classic text *Staying Power: The History of Black People in Britain* (London: Pluto Press, 1984) by Peter Fryer to make sense of our transatlantic migrations and Black identity. Books such as these that reckon with Black presence in Roman-occupied England and Black Liverpool show us that there are other ports of entry and temporalities of Black being in the British Isles. My dad also taught me about the strategic essentialism of Black as a political identity that people of non-white origin, Africans, Afro-West Indians, Asian, and Middle Eastern people rallied under in Afro-Asian solidarity. Chinese and East Asian presence more broadly has always posed a challenge to the matrix of British racialisation. Caribbean Chinese presence or Jamaican Chinese presence is even more perplexing for the British order of race.

So to imagine Hyacinth an Afro-Chinese woman from Jamaica in 1950s London is to imagine the impossible. Some of her photos are stamped with the mark of the photo studio, 'ROUGH PROOF PLEASE RETURN'. Did she pose for these photos at the now iconic Harry Jacobs studio where my father and his family posed for photos in Lambeth in the 1960s and 1970s? I do not know if Hyacinth returned to Jamaica. Hyacinth was rumoured to have checked into a sanatorium in London, but her fate is unknown.

I sit with not knowing Hyacinth and what it means to have a fate unknown as a presumed 'mad woman'. There is a long genealogy of wild West Indian women: emblematic of the tradition is Bertha, who burns down the English country manor in Charlotte Brontë's *Jane Eyre* (London: Smith, Elder & Co., 1847). Jean Rhys, who wrote from the perspective of Bertha, renamed her Antoinette in her novel *Wide Sargasso Sea* (London: André Deutsch, 1966); Rhys herself was an unruly West Indian woman, a white woman, also coming from the Caribbean, from Dominica to the UK when she was aged 16. Her life's work was a meditation on melancholia and the hysteric trope of the so-called mad West Indian woman.

Rhys lived a life bound by what scholar Donette Francis calls the 'sexual grammar' of the European colonial literary tradition. Francis describes Chinese women as 'protected', Indian women as 'policed', and Black women as 'untamed' in this calculus. What of the Afro-Chinese woman in this colonial fiction of group differentiation? Jean Rhys was haunted by the rigid grammar of what it meant to be a white woman, a third-generation creole white woman, in other words, by what it meant to be proximate to Blackness in the plantation order. White creole women were imagined to be wanton nymphomaniacs, as depicted in *Wide Sargasso Sea*. Extending this genealogy of diasporic Caribbean womanhood, I wonder how Hyacinth was sexualised when she arrived in the UK as an unmarried woman. I tread carefully in my speculation about the fate of women sent to sanatoriums, institutionalised women, heartbroken women, for any number of reasons, but the act alone is important.

There is an archive of forlorn women, childless women, perhaps by choice or maybe they wanted children. They are the aunties.

They are all but scratched out of the family tree. Hysteric, these women's crime was womanhood, afflicted with the 'physical disorder of women attributed to displacement or dysfunction of the uterus'. The wayward West Indian woman becomes an aberration, to be scratched out, or a cautionary tale.

In Figure 8.1, Hyacinth is the picture of a 1950s 'modern' woman. She is dressed in a prim and proper manner, with requisite modern accessories that speak to her comportment as a model subject. Her hair is bobbed, styled and coiffed just so. Written on the front of the photos, on the white border, in the same handwriting in blue ink are the dates, 1948, 1959, 1952, 1954. The full date is written on the back of some of the images. Whoever wrote

Figure 8.1 Hyacinth Lee, studio portrait, 1950s, United Kingdom. (Photo courtesy of Tao Leigh Goffe)

the dates imagined a future audience, imagined questions and wanted to provide clues, certainty of time and place. Perhaps they could not imagine a public, an audience, beyond the immediate family that would not know who Hyacinth was.

In one image, marked 1958, Hyacinth poses in front of a London Victorian brick house (Figure 8.2). It recalls for me the stakes of British real estate, racial enclosure, and how Caribbean 'arrivants', to use Kamau Brathwaite's term, were not permitted loans by banks or to rent and live wherever they wished. She is wrapped in a white shawl, probably to keep warm in London as much as a matter of style and propriety, not showing her bare arms. Her affect sometimes vibrant and sometimes uncertain,

Figure 8.2 Hyacinth Lee posing outside a house, 1958, United Kingdom. (Photo courtesy of Tao Leigh Goffe)

her hands in white gloves, Hyacinth's purse drapes off her wrist. In a similar image, marked 1956, we see Hyacinth with another woman, perhaps a friend, in front of a wooden picket fence (see Figure 8.3). They are coloured in neon green. So different from the

Figure 8.3 Scanned assorted photographs of Hyacinth Lee, 1950s. (Photo courtesy of Tao Leigh Goffe)

architecture of the Caribbean, the terrace houses and hedges ordered life and what it meant to be middle-class. In another image, from 1955, Hyacinth is pictured on a large steamship (see Figure 8.3). A man stands in the background holding what might be an oar. She looks happy here.

In another image, we see Hyacinth the bridesmaid; as far as I have gathered, she was never the bride. In another snapshot, she stands by palm fronds in 1955. The mystery photographer captures Hyacinth sitting on a cylindrical piece of machinery in an open field in 1948. Arranged next to these photos in the scanned album page is a studio portrait of my grandfather as a teenage boy in Hong Kong, leaning up next to his stepmother, an elderly woman, seated. This placement, this logic of curation of the family album, suggests to me that Hyacinth knew of her brother Edwin. The intimacy of siblings who would never meet but knew of each other is common in Caribbean families that stretch across continents. He or his stepmother would have sent this photograph from Hong Kong, and it was cherished, at least enough to be preserved, arranged in an album, and housed in Miami in 2017. Though Edwin did not know them, his kin knew him.

Edith Clarke's classic text *My Mother Who Fathered Me: A Study of the Families in Three Selected Communities in Jamaica* (Mona, Jamaica: University of West Indies Press, 1997) works to dispel assumptions from the 1950s about post-slavery plantation societies and how this rendered West Indian family trees. *Family in the Caribbean* (Oxford, UK: J. Currey, 1996) by Christine Barrow is a modern edition, part of this body of literature. Fernando Henriques wrote of the matriarchal dynamic in post-slavery societies and its pathologising effect in *Family and Colour in Jamaica* (London: Eyre & Spottiswoode, 1953). The pathologising of the Black family as a problem to be fixed in the wake of slavery is endless. The historic pathologising of the Black woman is endless. She is blamed for the failure of the

Black family, as Black feminist critic Hortense Spillers famously dissected against the Moynihan Report.

The Black woman is a problem cast as an 'irresponsible reproducer', and she is still a problem when she is childless, a ravenous, mad Jamaican woman to be locked away in the attic. If I had been looking for Hyacinth, I am sure I would never have found her. She is locked away by the opacity of what I cannot know. A subject born of the convergence of Africa and China in the Americas, determined by the racial enclosure of the plantation and metropolitan ghetto, Hyacinth found me. In seeking her, I am not interested in furthering the field of inquiry some have called Critical Mixed-Race Studies, but rather in the question of colonial entanglement of the Black diaspora and the overseas Chinese.

I caught eyes with her. Over the years, I have seen glimpses of her – a Black woman, also of Chinese heritage – in novels, anthropological writings, Hollywood musicals, newspaper reportage and beauty pageantry. I have also seen traces of her distant cousin in Latin America and South America – Peru, Panama and Brazil. In Cuba, she is called *la mulata achinada*.[2] In Suriname, she is known as *blaka sneisi*.[3] The Black Chinese woman appears and reappears in a series of disappearing acts. She represents the entangled political economies of racial slavery and racial indenture, enacted in spite of the violent order of European coloniality. My fate is her fate. The surface of the photograph is what I have. The digital materiality of an illuminated screen is my portal to another Windrush.

The scar tissue of the flesh of indenture is what we are left with as the surface of the family photo. The scratch marks form coded

---

2 See the considerable research on *la mulata achinada* in Martin Tsang (ed.), *Afro-Asian Connections in Latin America and the Caribbean* (Lanham, MD: Lexington Books, 2019).

3 See Paul Brendan Tjon Sie Fat's extensive research on the tension between heterogeneous communities of Chinese migrants in Suriname and its diaspora, *Chinese New Migrants in Suriname* (Amsterdam, the Netherlands: University of Amsterdam, 2009).

hieroglyphics of opacity that I will never know. The generational trauma of silenced women could have rendered Hyacinth a No Name Woman, like the deliberately forgotten Chinese women of Maxine Hong Kingston's writing. It strikes me that as much as we are told about how bound and confined women were during the early and mid-twentieth century, there are plenty of examples of women who wandered and travelled alone, wayward women, to echo Saidiya Hartman. There were women like Hyacinth who determined their own itineraries, often without husbands or fathers.

When I read Jamaican philosopher Sylvia Wynter's narration of her life, born in 1928 in Cuba, I hear this wandering and independence. In an early pursuit of the metropole and a life in the arts, Wynter began her career as a dancer and an actress. Wynter's biography is an Atlantic itinerary of a womanhood from Cuba to Jamaica to the United Kingdom. Wynter received degrees in Modern Languages in 1949 and Spanish in 1953 from King's College, London. She travelled across Europe, marrying a Norwegian pilot before returning to Jamaica, then Sweden, and then the United States. I recognise the itinerary of Canadian Trinidadian Chinese filmmaker Richard Fung's cousin Nang (b. 1934), who narrates just such a story of modern womanhood and adventure in the 1950s and 1960s. Nang, who is Afro-Chinese-Indigenous (Amerindian) Trinidadian, leads the viewer on a cinematic journey through her life story in Fung's documentary *Nang by Nang* (2019), a still from which can be seen in Figure 8.4. Nang, like Wynter, was a dancer. She was choreographed by the famous Trinidadian actor and dancer Geoffrey Holder. She later trained to become a nurse. Nang was married and divorced many times, had six husbands, and travelled the world from Trinidad to London to Venezuela to New York in the 1940s. So perhaps the itinerary of wayward West Indian women, modern Black women in the 1950s, was much more common than we are accustomed to believing, and the metropole, London, was a pivotal stop along the way. The process of forgetting women like Hyacinth and Nang works through the processes of historiography.

Figure 8.4   Still from *Nang by Nang* (Dir. Richard Fung, 2019). (Reprinted with the artist's permission)

An answer towards remembering lies in the juncture where oral history meets art, as performed by photographer Albert Chong, who is of Afro-Chinese heritage. He touches on the theme of silenced women's narratives inscribed on the photographic surface. In his work of art *Aunt Winnie*, he honorifically positions his aunt, who was of Afro-Chinese heritage too, as a subject beyond colonial history. Chong wrote 'The Sisters and Aunt Winnie'[4] to address and caption his photographic collages that draw from his Jamaican Chinese family album.

Chong scratches the surface of family albums in his series of photographic collages that depict Winnifred Lynn, his aunt. His works of art draw on excerpts his sister, Marie Sang Demato, recorded from an oral history interview with their aunt. Chong overlays Winnie's words on her portrait from the 1950s (Figure 8.5). The story is one of the mystery of Aunt Winnie losing her one true love, Dadda. In another image, Chong inscribes the oral

---

4   A chapter in Marianne Hirsch (ed.), *The Familial Gaze* (Hanover, NH: University Press of New England, 1999).

history on a copper mat that frames her image (Figure 8.6). He etches her story into the pliable metal surface. Hieroglyphics of the flesh, to use Hortense Spillers' poetic phrase, are carved into the family photo album in Chong's aesthetic process. The flesh of family is fleshy like the uterus, and this is significant as we learn from the oral history that Aunt Winnie did not have children. She was not able to. She did not love her husband, but tried to tolerate being sexually intimate with him. Winnie had contemplated adopting Albert Chong's sister. The photo album alone cannot tell this story, so we must let Winnifred narrate for herself, like Nang. In this absence for Hyacinth, I am left with the speculative mode.

'She left Jamaica to forget him,' writes Chong of Aunt Winnie. Simple as the heartbreak and the forlorn fragments of

Figure 8.5 Aunt Winnie's Story' (1996) by Albert Chong. (Reprinted with the artist's permission)

Figure 8.6 'Aunt Winnie' (1996) by Albert
Chong. (Reprinted with the artist's permission)

Aunt Winnie's story may be, they gesture to the dark circuitry
of Afro-Chinese life in the 1950s between continents, of inside
and outside children. The horizontal relation of family provided
support in the wake of so many parents who left and may never
have returned in Caribbean families, whether to London or
Spanish Guiana (Venezuela). Siblings lived in different hemi-
spheres without much knowledge of each other's fates or
trajectories, like my maternal grandfather and his sister Hyacinth.
It strikes me that the process of forgetting these hysteric or mel-
ancholic childless women like Hyacinth is the same sort of cyclic
colonial forgetting of Afro-Asian relationality. It needs rein-
venting time and again, though there is a history of African and
Asian people labouring side by side in various moments through

time. So I imagine Hyacinth living her last days in London, with these photographs of her arrival and departure. She is the Other Windrush that cannot be accommodated by a nostalgic TV docudrama or the neat periodising of the timeline of coloniality. Almost hand-tinted, perhaps Hyacinth herself coloured the photographs, scratching the surface of the film, to render life how it replayed in her memory: not monochromatic, but in full colour.

9

Everything of Us

Maria del Pilar Kaladeen

Since my mother died, I have been travelling for four hours one day a week, out of London and back again. I had become aware that my dad was, as he put it, 'fading away'. Unable to handle his paperwork, inclined to forget what needed to be done and housebound as the result of problems balancing. On the last occasion he went to the city centre, he ambulated so precariously that the police, on seeing him, arranged for two paramedics to take him home. Even with the knowledge that he is approaching his 82nd year, the idea of my dad walking unsteadily is something I am still getting accustomed to. Since the early 1980s he had worked in London's best hotels as a silver service waiter. The weight of the trays he carried so easily in and out of ballrooms in order to feed his five children would have been immense to anyone else. But this job, that gave him no time to think, was what he most wanted: to be so tired that he could automatically shut down any voice that told him that he had failed, that he couldn't have travelled thousands of miles across a frigid ocean

> to an ice-cold bedsit,
> to live amongst a lukewarm people,
> to become a waiter?

He would come home late at night, quietly removing his shoes at the entrance to the house, as he must have done in Guyana as a boy. His bow tie would be untied, but still around his neck, his waistcoat still done up. He would remove the tools of his trade from his pockets: bottle opener, cigar cutter, pen. He would have been aware each night he came home to the house that he had not, in any sense, lived up to his father's dreams for him.

His father, my grandfather, was the last of ten children of an indentured labourer named Kalidin who arrived in British Guiana in 1881. Born in 1915, he was named Beharry, and he was the only one of his siblings to avoid a working life on the plantation. Beharry was apprenticed to another Indian-Guyanese from whom he learnt the skill of tailoring, eventually opening his own shop in Georgetown. He was a forward-thinking man who educated his daughters as well as his sons and who wanted more for his children. It was Beharry who anglicised our family name from 'Kalidin' to 'Kaladeen', keen that we should not be associated with the colonially acquired stain of Kali worship and that Indianness, while important to him, should not be the thing that held his children back.

I understand that my grandfather was loved unreservedly by his children and respected in his community. On a monthly basis, he would make his home a dharamsala by feeding those who were needy in the community. In the heat of the Indian–African race riots of the 1960s, Beharry moved his family to Canada, where two of my father's siblings had already settled. He accepted this new world and its colour bars without complaint. He took work as a doorman at the Hotel Fairmont and set to picking up the pieces of his life as the shepherd of the family. Guyanese people are not always generous with their words; however, I have never met one who said anything negative about my grandfather. His reputation as a good and kind man was sealed by his early death, at 56, of an aneurysm. My father's brothers and sisters were crushed by this loss, which was made greater by the knowledge that they had not lived up to his educational expectations for them. But it was my dad, the second eldest, who left not just Guyana, but his entire family, who felt the death less and the sense of having disappointed him more.

In the weeks after my mother died, my father spoke to me about his daily journey from his house to Peter's Hall primary school, grudgingly created by the colonial planters to educate the children on the plantation of the same name. Beharry, had gone to the same school as a boy and had the same teacher. This teacher, 'Teacher Solomon', would look at my dad fixedly at least once a week, and with the firm conviction that the intellectual apple had fallen far from the tree, she would say to him, wagging her finger and shaking her head, 'Boy, you're nothing like your father.' In many of our conversations, we would return to this walk to school and to the people and events of this time, and it was in the telling and the retelling of these stories that he seemed sometimes to finally understand that my mother, who he had asked for intermittently since her death, was not coming back.

Things had been bad between my parents in the months before my mother died. In the hospital, she refused to see him. There was nothing irregular in this. In over 55 years of marriage, they had never managed to find a way to live together without conflict. In the weeks after the ambulance brought him home, he stopped going out. The little he did to help out in the house dwindled away to nothing, and she became responsible for every single meal, washed plate and hoovered carpet. He retreated into himself. She would call me, angry, resentful, hinting darkly that she had concerns about her own health. Eventually, they stopped talking to each other, a pattern that they had established during my childhood when one furious bust-up could lead to years of silence. For the majority of my school years, they did not talk at all, but my older brothers remember a time when things were different, when they would occasionally communicate without friction. But they also remember having to physically come between them. If I try, I too remember these moments. I can see the pieces of her

radio scattered on a carpet because he smashed it. In that Nean-
derthal way he had

of letting her know
that he was the boss,
and she was nothing.

My parents were the sort of people who should have been very
particular about whom they married and how many children they
had. My mother, a fair-haired, blue-eyed Galician from the north
of Spain, should have settled for someone as white and glacial as
herself. Then she would have not spent the remaining decades
of her life blaming her husband's 'culture' and her children's
mixedness for the mess of her life. And my father should definitely not have had five children; he hated noise and he hated
disorder, and in that singular Caribbean way, he believed that dis-
cipline was something that could be whacked into a child. Perhaps
he should have married a woman lighthearted enough not to
always take him literally, who understood the Guyanese need to
perform, that what we say is not necessarily true. That sometimes
it is more about how it sounds. That words and their meanings
can sometimes have separate lives. But my mother was born in
the Spanish Civil War and grew up in a dictatorship. She did not
come from a time or place where hearts could afford to be 'light'.

There had been signs before. But they are never really signs
before, are they? In truth, they become what we have decided to
see after the fact. It was difficult to tell if his memory had dete-
riorated after his first stroke. 'He has always been absentminded,'
we would say. This absentmindedness had cost my mother hours
of worry when they first married. She did not work outside the
home, and my father assumed total financial responsibility for the
family. She developed a habit of going through the papers on his
desk to check that bills were paid. Each time she was pregnant,
she lived in fear that he would one day walk out of a shop and

forget to pay for something. She need not have worried. He knew his limitations and never walked into a large shop without picking up a basket, knowing his capacity, even when young, to get lost in his own head. When they were courting, my dad confided in my mum that he had gone out on a date with a girl and left her in the middle of London to go home, completely forgetting he had been with her until he reached his bedsit. My mum was born in the same region of Spain as María Pita, spear-carrying vanquisher of the English invaders, she would have stared him straight into an understanding that he would never forget her. In the years following his first stroke, she would be momentarily preoccupied about him. 'He gets very confused,' she would say, but she didn't take it further and I didn't press her. I wondered if this 'confusion' was just his way of shutting her down.

Three months after she died, I arrived at the house and began to make coffee. My back was to him, so he didn't see my face when he asked me where 'mummy' was.

'You don't remember?' There was a long pause.

'I remember,' he said eying me, as though I didn't have all the facts. 'But I can hear her sometimes, moving around up there.' With his head he gestured to the room above us that had always been hers. There was a moderate sense of triumph in his voice, like when you're right but you don't want to gloat. The next morning, I called the doctor, and two days later I received a call back. My father had been diagnosed with dementia four-and-a-half years ago, they said, was I sure he had not told anyone?

What did he do? Did he walk out of the clinic and decide not to tell anyone? Did he walk out of the clinic and forget his diagnosis? Did he walk out of the clinic and decide that he did not accept the diagnosis? I do remember that a couple of decades ago, he told me, with real fear in his eyes, that his grandmother, had 'something like' dementia before she died in her early eighties. This woman, Butchia, had come to Guyana as a little girl with her mother in 1876, and eventually became Kalidin's wife. Whatever he decided that day, my mum died thinking that my dad had retreated into himself and ignored her own declining health. She never told him about the mass that she must have known was growing inside her. By the time she went to the doctor, her undiagnosed cancer had metastasised, and within two weeks of arriving at the hospital, she was dead. Right up until the last moment, she had refused to see him and so the marriage ended as it had endured: on the back of misunderstandings and nurtured grudges.

Inevitably, we have become time travellers in our weekly conversations. We talk a lot about that journey to his primary school in Guyana along the road that ran past the cane field. We talk about how he used to follow the road back home at lunchtime and see his uncles, Kalidin's sons, and employees of the plantation peacefully engaged in their lunch. He told me that he had not wanted to disturb them as they looked so grateful for their break.

'Why? What would they have said?'

'Oh, you know, "Come here, boy."'

He says this in a gruff, affectionate way that I recognise immediately as the way he speaks to his grandsons.

But of course, he is getting worse. His mind will not miraculously fuse itself back together, and he will lose more of his memories. One day, quite recently, I told him that I was sorry that he never had an opportunity to share conversations like this with his own father.

'You were so young when you lost him,' I said.

'My dad's not dead,' he said shaking his head, looking at me surprised.

Two weeks later, he called me to ask what time his father was coming home from work. When I tried to find out more, I understood that in his mind, the day before, his father, my mother and I had all been in the house with him. But now he was alone and he did not know why.

This is how I understand what is happening to him. Time is not linear, and he sees everything of himself and his past together.

In this way, nobody is dead and it is possible that he can be sitting in the room with his grandson, wondering when his own father will get back from work. Each week, as we travel along the road to Peter's Hall primary school, it feels as though we have moved a little further back in time, as though we are heading back to the beginning of that first day when he stepped out of the door to head off to school.

My father has never spent a night in hospital, and one of the nurses who visits him at home told me this naturally makes him a terrible patient: he is unused to being unwell and has never taken medicine. Once, he was very seriously ill, but he does not remember this. When he was no more than a toddler, he had what would probably now be diagnosed as bronchiolitis. I know this because my uncle, my father's older brother, told me that he remembered their maternal grandfather, Swantimala, a striking-

Figure 9.1   Maria del Pilar Kaladeen's South Indian great-grandfather, Swantimala. (Photograph courtesy of the Kaladeen family collection)

looking South Indian man who spoke Tamil, coming to the house and asking his daughter, my grandmother, to let him take care of him. He took my dad away, and returned him days later when he had recovered. I loved this story because it encapsulated the wonder of extended family that I had never known in London. As a child, my father grew up with all but one of his grandparents; only Kalidin had died before he was born. I imagine this man – handsome, dark-skinned and grey-haired – striding off down the road with my dad in his arms and his daughter, looking on, safe in the knowledge that he could make everything right.

In the coming months, he will forget many more things. But I hope that some fragment of this story about his grandfather will remain. The story of a man who loved his daughter, a daughter who trusted her father, and a child held secure and certain in the land of his birth, peaceful and unaware of all that he would one day leave behind.

10

Three Rivers

Mr Gee

In 1996, I was a carefree young man in my early twenties, I was visiting Port of Spain, Trinidad to immerse myself in the two-day exhaustion known as Carnival. The song that was on everyone's lips at the time was '*Jahaji Bhai* – Brotherhood of the Boat' by Brother Marvin.

Now, I wasn't Trinidadian, nor was I ever really a big calypso fan. I grew up on London's cold streets, where any sound that reminded you of sunshine was greeted with scepticism. I first encountered this unique song at a competition show on Dimanche Gras (Carnival Sunday). This is when they crown the Carnival King and Queen and all the top performers attend in the hope of winning that coveted prize. After sitting through several acts, whose names have all escaped me, the singer I was waiting for, Brother Marvin, came out in front of a huge, roaring crowd. Dressed in a splendid white and gold outfit, the stage lights flattered his flowing robes; he moved with purpose, and seemed to capture an unseen breeze. He was every inch a calypso star: a charismatic Black man, larger than life, deep chocolate skin, original broad nose and dark curls in his hair. He looked like me, and having heard so much about this song, I was desperate to see it performed in front of a live audience.

When he grabbed the mic and proceeded to perform, the people went berserk, and I understood why. Every syllable of every word of his song bounced around inside my head as I heard something that I had never heard in my life before:

So it is ah great privilege
To have such unique heritage
Fifty percent Africa, fifty percent India.

What did this guy just say? Had he actually written a song
drawing on his heritage from two of the oldest peoples on the
earth? Was he really referring to the toxic voyages that brought
both Africans and Indians into the Caribbean? Was he trying to
find a commonality between slavery and indentureship, and were
the crowd actually cheering him on? I couldn't believe it, because
'Jahaji Bhai' wasn't a typical 'jump up, jump up, party-party' song,
and yet here everyone was, dancing and singing along. I wished
that my friends Ollie and Brian back in London were here to
see this, it would blow their minds. I listened in disbelief to this
unique plea for Black and brown unity, so eloquently expressed,
so powerfully delivered, such a convincing sentiment But did I
believe a word of it? Fuck, no!

Like the great Brother Marvin, I have that 'unique heritage': 50
per cent African and 50 per cent Indian. My mother was born in
Guyana and is of Indian heritage; my father was born in Uganda
and is of African heritage. Meanwhile, I was born in England, the
land that had once colonised both of these countries, so although
Uganda and Guyana are totally different, my parents both grew
up singing 'God Save the Queen' and drinking Milo, albeit on
different sides of the Atlantic. Both countries achieved their independence from Britain during the 1960s, so both of my parents
got to witness and compare pre- and post-colonial realities. As a
result of the British system of indenture, each country also has a
sizeable Indian population living alongside a sizeable African population (in Uganda the Africans are the majority, while in Guyana
the Indians are the majority). Putting it mildly, relations between
these two communities in both countries have been traumatic.

'Jahaji Bhai' spoke to me because it described an uncomfortable divide that I had become accustomed to, and up until that

day in 1996, I had never heard anyone articulate a reality that was so close my own personal truth. I look completely African, though, you would have to look hard to find evidence of any mix. In Guyana, all of my family are Indian, in Uganda all of my family are Black. I have African relations who despise Indians and Indian relations who despise Africans, yet we all go quiet in front of white people.

'If you go with Black woman, look at how dark your children will be.'

'If you go with an Indian man, they'll make sure to cut you out of their family tree.'

'Mind those Black guys don't rob you on the block.'

'Mind that Indian man doesn't rob you in his shop.'

'We hate them, because they hate us.'

'We hate them, because they hate us.'

'We hate them, because they hate us.'

'Ssssshhhhhh, white people are coming.'

'Besides, nobody can cook rice like we.'

This is the game that we play. Outside the white gaze, Black and Indian communities like to pull each other apart, it's our sport to find new names and new ways to look down on each other.

Five years earlier, England, 1991: I was at Ollie's house in Streatham, the hang-out spot, neutral ground. Ollie was a good friend of mine: he was white and an only child, born and bred in South London. Unfortunately, his parents were in the throes of splitting up, as they were divorcing. It was an ugly time for all involved. Ollie was often at home alone, and in order to assuage their guilt, both parents used to shower him with gifts and let him do what he liked. So Ollie had the latest clothes, the newest shoes, the shiniest watch, the best weed and a new Nintendo game system. This pretty much made his house a mecca for every teenager desperate to escape their own drab bedrooms.

One day, I was at Ollie's, listening to the current chapter of his disintegrating household, when the doorbell rang. Ollie went downstairs to open it, and a tall Indian guy rushed in, quite fair-skinned, with his hair gelled and slicked back to look like a young Michael Corleone. After *Godfather* and *Scarface* came on TV, every Indian kid that I met was trying to pass himself off as Al Pacino. We used to call them 'Al Patels'. Anyway, this guy stormed upstairs, burst into Ollie's room where I was sitting, and paused briefly in the doorway to catch his breath. Ollie slowly followed up behind him, smiling that gormless middle-class white boy smile, as if to say his circle of ethnic friends was now complete.

It must have been raining outside because this guy's jacket was wet, and to my annoyance, he threw himself down onto the remaining space of the couch right next to me and with a panicked yell shouted at Ollie: 'Quick, bro, turn the TV on, turn the TV on, BBC1 ... quick!' Ollie calmly picked up the remote control, switched off the game I was playing, and changed the channel to the regular TV. To be honest, this annoyed me even further, because I was clocking up quite a high score and was damn near the final level. Al Patel had fucked up my game. Now, I know that this was Ollie's house, but I felt like this new dude was encroaching on my space.

To break the ice, Ollie rushed through rudimentary introductions: 'Hey, Brian, this is Gee. Gee, this is Brian, me and him work at Blockbuster together, I told him to pass through.' 'Brian?' I thought to myself, 'I've never met an Indian guy called Brian.' 'So what's the rush, Bri?', I said (shortening his name on purpose). 'What exactly are we looking for on the TV?' With his eyes full of excitement, seemingly hypnotised by the TV screen, Brian uttered the five words that would enlighten us all: 'It's Michael Jackson's new video!'

A hush filled the room. These were the days before YouTube and before social media, where if a new video was broadcast, you did not know when it would come on the TV again. Ollie adjusted the control, and a new sound filled the room. For the next five minutes, the three of us were engrossed in Michael Jackson's new video for his single 'Black or White'. You know the one, it is his call for racial harmony as he dances with all the different people of the world accompanied by Slash playing on guitar. Meanwhile, a young Macaulay Culkin, sporting dark shades and a huge gold chain, delivers the immortal rap: 'I'm not going to spend my life being a colour'. The scene then shifts to a solo shot of a brown man who then morphs into a Black woman, who then morphs into a white woman who then keeps on morphing. 'Morphing' was the new word (as we would discover later) to describe this transformative process of blending appearances, which continues towards the video's ending: multiple transformations made between different races and genders, thus hammering Michael's point home. Boom, mic-drop! It's a visual game-changer.

Of course, the sentiment of the slick Hollywood video was not lost upon the diverse trio viewing it in that tiny bedroom in South London. This was 1991; I was Black, Ollie was white, and Brian was brown. Despite the snapshot of unity that the three of us represented, we were all well aware that our city of birth was quite divided. This aside, we appreciated that 'Black or White' was an impressive piece of film:

'Rah, did you see the way those faces changed colour? That was deep!'

'It was seamless, I've never seen anything like it.'

'Yup, MJ's back in the building!'

'That rap was kind of crap, though.'

Wanting to capture the mood of the moment, Ollie started to ponder about identity in the clunky way that only a stoned white kid from England can. 'If only it were so easy to jump between the races,' he remarked, 'You know what? I don't mean to sound racist, but I think I'd make a pretty good Black man.'

'Oh, you think so?', snapped back Brian, waving his hands in an instant dismissal, as if to part the sea of smoke that had embraced us all, 'The police would have raided this place a long time ago if you were! Ha, I'm closer to being Black than you are.' Brian then put his right hand close to mine, and with his left hand he rubbed that flat area of skin just above his wrist, to emphasise the point that he was on my side. He then gestured at me for approval. I looked at him with incredulity.

'What the fuck do any of you know about being Black? Brian, even MJ is lighter than you nowadays, so what does he know?' Ollie laughed hysterically. I guess that between the smoke and the tension, he found our interracial bickering funny, but Brian wasn't laughing at all. In fact, his tone turned serious.

'Well, that's where you're wrong, Gee. My mother's Black.'

A second hush had now entered the room. 'What are you on about Brian?', said Ollie, 'I always thought that you were Indian, isn't your last name Ramjit or something like that?'

'Yeah, my father's Indian, but my mum's Black. Ramjit is my dad's surname ... well, actually, he's not from India-India, he's from Guyana. That's where both my parents are from. So I look more like my father, but my mother looks more like Gee.'

Ollie's head must have started spinning as he leaned slightly forwards as if to get a better look at his friend. 'Are you taking the piss, mate? ... Where are you really from?'

Suddenly I too felt emboldened. 'Seriously, Brian? I can't lie, when I first saw you, I thought that you were "Indian-Indian". I can't believe that your folks are from Guyana? That's where my mother's from, she's Indian, almost as light as you. But my dad's from Uganda, East Africa, and I look more like him.'

There was nothing in that Michael Jackson video that could explain to Ollie what he had just heard. The third hush belonged to him, and him alone. His Black friend had turned out to be half-brown, and his brown friend had turned out to be half-Black, plus it seemed that nobody was going to explain to him what 'Indian-Indian' meant.

For the rest of the evening, the three of us were on a voyage of discovery. It was the first time that I had ever met anyone else who was half-Indian, half-Black, just like me. I'm pretty sure that it was the same for Brian. We were the same, yet we looked completely different. Talking to Brian that night opened my eyes. Even though Brian and I shared similar heritage, even though we both grew up in the same city at the same time, it was the difference in our appearance that defined the lives that we led. We had chosen to live our lives as colours.

Brian identified as Indian, and I identified as Black, we were both raised by mothers that we did not resemble. Racial identity did not exist inside the home, but it was always there once you stepped outside. We both grew up in London as children of immigrants in the 1970s and 80s. As children of immigrants amidst other children of immigrants, we had to choose a tribe. Brian had found his tribe among the South Asian community in Southall. Southall was well known throughout the UK as 'little India', it was a place where white racists had repeatedly been chased out of town. These victories brought confidence to the community living there. Nobody fucked with them, and so for Brian, it felt like a good place to call home.

He told us that hanging out in Southall made him wish that he was fully Indian, so that he could fit in with the friends that he had made there. Brian went to daytime bhangra raves, dated Asian girls and even picked up a few words of Gujarati slang, but every Christmas he would be at midnight mass with his mother. He knew how to walk the line, none of his Indian friends would have guessed that his mother was Black. Maintaining this appearance would often result in Brian deliberately turning a blind eye to derogatory comments his Indian friends made about Black people. He simply ignored them or smiled along. After all, this was just schoolyard banter and they were not really referring to *his* mother, were they? But the waves that accompanied the Atlantic slave ships still had a grave hold on his mind. I recognised his story. Brian did not need to justify anything to me; it was about survival, acceptance, friendship and the knowledge that the tribes that we had chosen, did not have much love for each other.

Meanwhile, I found my tribe among the Black community in Brixton. It was where I gravitated. It had the best hip-hop and reggae shops, the best pirate radio stations, the best buzz of excitement and the funniest characters. Brixton was the capital of Black Britain, this was where Muhammad Ali, Nelson Mandela and Mike Tyson had visited; it was where Mr Gee the poet was born. Like Brian, I chose the tribe who looked like me. Brixton also held a homogenised view of the Black experience which you had to accept in order to be accepted, it was largely Jamaican. But Black music was the lingua franca, and this knowledge allowed you to navigate its pathways. I picked up more American and Jamaican slang than I ever did Guyanese or Ugandan. I knew more about the US civil rights movement than I did about the indentureship of my Indian ancestors. I too have had to turn a blind eye when my Black friends have made derogatory comments about Indians. After all, I wanted to fit in; I convinced myself that they weren't talking about my mother. Besides, she was Guyanese-Indian, she wasn't Indian Indian.

Meeting Brian was a relief. I could understand that he was as African as he was Indian. He could understand that I was as Indian as I was African. It was something that neither of us had ever denied, but also something that we rarely mentioned within our own tribes.

At one point, Ollie asked us both: 'Well where do you see yourselves as coming from?' I motioned to the window, opened up the curtain ever so slightly, and pointed my finger through the newly formed divide. To which Ollie responded, 'London?'

'No,' I said, 'Outside.'

Brian nodded in agreement.

When Black and South Asian communities display racism towards one another, it's not the same as when white people are being racist towards them. No, our hatred goes unchecked and is shared without remorse. There is no equivalent of 'liberal white guilt'. Brian knew that to constantly declare himself as half-Black would mark him as someone uncomfortable with his brown skin. Just as I knew that to declare myself as half-brown would mark me as someone uncomfortable with my black skin. This was 30 years before Kamala Harris's rise to Vice President of the United States. Unlike in Guyana and Trinidad, the term 'mixed' has only one implication in the UK: that somebody in your family is white or 'Somebody married up.' This was the only mixture that anyone was prepared to engage with at that time.

In 2018, the editors of this anthology and their colleagues at Senate House Library commissioned me to write a poem to reflect on the centenary of the birth of the Indian-Guyanese politician Cheddi Jagan. It was going to be part of an annual conference on the study of indentureship. In researching my poem, I was given access to the library's archive on Guyana. My final piece, 'A Tale of Three Rivers', was originally intended to be a reflection on the life of the Guyanese politician Cheddi Jagan. Jagan was a child of indenture, a son of India who stood up to the British and the Americans in his fight for his country's freedom. Growing up in an Indian-Guyanese household, I was well aware of his name, his cause and his tribe. But how can anyone speak about the politics of Cheddi Jagan without mentioning Forbes Burnham? A child of slavery, a son of Africa. A different name, a different cause, a different tribe. They were two close friends who eventually became enemies. It's a story that speaks to a divide that I've known all of my life – Indian against African – so the poem about Cheddi became my own tale of indenture: a story that is British, Indian and African. The stories are all connected inside me, in the same way that rivers are all connected inside oceans. I now finally understand the sentiment behind that song by Brother Marvin that I had originally scoffed at. It is a great privilege to have such unique heritage: 50 per cent Africa, 50 per cent India.

A TALE OF THREE RIVERS

They call it the 'Land of many waters'
But here's a tale of three rivers,
How they intertwine to reflect my life's many mirrors,

The River Ganges baptised my indentured heart,
While my ebony soul floated down the Nile,
But the River Thames partitioned them apart,
Before they could put the West on trial,[1]

Water nah get enemy,[2]
But I'm yet to see Jahaji Bhai,[3]
So I now speak the language found in the colour of my teardrops,

You see, I'm half-African & half-Guyanese Indian,
My system's filled with two waters and a violence,
That saturates both traditions,

I grew up in London:
And between the 70s and 80s,
I was toasted by Guyanese whispers poured,
out onto family tables,
By uncles who harboured inebriated blisters,
From Windrushed[4] trips to echoed graveyards,
Candlelit shots of El Dorado,[5]
Golden Cities lost in split suggestions;

---

1   *The West on Trial: My Fight for Guyana's Freedom* (London: Michael Joseph, 1966) – Cheddi Jagan's autobiographical work.
2   'Water No Get Enemy' – a 1975 song by Nigerian musician Fela Kuti.
3   *'Jahaji Bhai'* – a 1996 song by Trinidadian musician Brother Marvin.
4   *Empire Windrush* – the ship that brought one the first large groups of post-war West Indian immigrants to the United Kingdom in 1948.
5   El Dorado – a lost city of gold, rumoured to be in Guyana. It is also the name of a local rum.

'Bwoy de first rule of di Plantation, is dey choke yuh
    Independence!'
'Den dey rob yuh at election'
'Beat yuh wid a rod of no correction'
'But yuh don't wanna ever be around when di cutlass slips'
'Yuh don't wanna ever 'ear di truth from di Pandit's lips'
'Just pass mi another drink Bwoy, and don't watch my sips'
'And as for this Winston Churchill cigar? ... It's superb!'[6]

Thus mumbled my drunk Indian uncle one Notting Hill night,
Over plates of Chinese food & spilt Madeira wine,
I laughed as he struggled to form a sentence from
    Pre-Columbian times,
For nobody at that table could speak their Mother's Tongue,

He saw my childish giggles drenched in English privilege,
For what did this little black boy from London know,
About the range or the village?
About the rape or the pillage?
The blood that sugar-cane delivers,
Son Chapman?[7] Wismar?[8]
These are names I can't envisage,
So with an emotional quickness ... he sobered up.

'Oh ... so yuh does laugh when we talk about Guyanese
    Freedom?'
'Yuh does t'ink England give Independence easy?'
'One flag dun, another flag raise?'
'Bwoy! yuh don't know about we punished and di price we
    paid ...'

---

6   In 1953, Winston Churchill dispatched the warship HMS *Superb*, laden with troops, to suspend British Guiana's constitution and arrest Cheddi Jagan.

7   *Son Chapman* was a vessel that sank on the Demerara river in 1964 due to explosions. Forty-three people died, all Black. The perpetrators remain unknown.

8   In the Wismar Massacre of 1964, rioting targeted the Indian minority living in this village. More than 3,000 Indians were evacuated after the riots.

'AFRICA and INDIA went to war!'

And like a jaguar's roar,
My peaceful waterfall was struck by this stumbling stone,
It rippled inside my bloodstream with self-destructive
    overload,
Indian arteries attacking my black veins,
African bones puncturing my brown lungs,
As the River Nile and the River Ganges fought to escape the
    lowest rung,[9]

Meanwhile by the River Thames,
We fed breadcrumbs to the swans,
And it was on this day in 1980
That I witnessed the true cost of Revolution,

My uncle spoke of a British-owned Guyana 1953,
Where the Booker[10] prize for fiction has to be seen to be
    believed,
He told me of two young men,
One called Forbes, One called Cheddi,
Who united to win their country's first Democratic election,

A child of India and a child of Africa sounding the thunder
    for Independence,
But Washington & Westminster can make paving stones of
    good intentions,
For History has a power and its power can form a weapon,
And Lord knows every weapon can be turned upon itself,

---

9 'Lowest Rung' – a chapter detailing racial unrest from the book *Trouble in Guyana* (London: Allen & Unwin, 1966) by Peter Simms.
10 The Booker family derived its wealth from the huge sugar plantations it owned in Guyana from the early nineteenth century onwards.

He told me that Africans died moving 100 million tonnes of
    dirt,
To mould Guyana's destiny[11] from the sea,
And Indian backs were put to work,
Plantation charm is sugar-sweet,
Amerindian land rights were dispersed,
By Whites, Chinese and Portuguese,
So for someone to reverse from all this hurt,
They gotta speak to all-a-we,

Because there's no point in shouting at the lock,
Unless your voice provides the key,
And Cheddi & Forbes found freedom's door handle was
    blocked,
By those who claimed democracy,
… But there were some things that they couldn't foresee,

Did they really think that the River Thames wants the River
    Nile and River Ganges to agree?
And include the River Amazon and re-join the sea of Liberty?
Did they not think that CIA and MI6 would split these rivers
    into streams?
If you can count the number of boats offering a 'better life in
    London',
You best count the number of the beast,

Now watch your streams proportioned into trickles,
As everybody wants to leave,
'Mummy, how can I take the Cold War to the store …
… when there's nothing left to eat?'

---

11   *A Destiny to Mould* (Harlow, UK: Longman, 1970) – a book of speeches by
Forbes Burnham.

Come see your trickles reduced to droplets,
Leaving you hungry in the streets,
Where the hatred of your neighbour,
Is the only religion you believe,

Finally let your droplets dictate your tears,
As election fever disappears,
I've seen Guyanese of all races drown their sorrows in
    London's pubs,
Two shots of rum for every beer,

They call it the Land of Many Waters,
But I can only speak of three rivers,
How they intertwine to reflect my life's mirrors,

Perhaps the legacy of Guyanese Independence is one that's yet
    to be defined,
Until the River Berbice, the River Essequibo, & River
    Demerara,[12]
Flow into our hearts and Free our minds.

---

12   Berbice, Essequibo and Demerara – the three largest rivers that run through
Guyana.

11

Interview:
'Invited then Unwelcomed'

Charlotte Bailey

This is an oral history interview with Charlotte Bailey, conducted by Maria del Pilar Kaladeen on 15 January 2021.

Charlotte, I know that your grandfather was Indian-Trinidadian. Can I ask you what you know about him?

My grandma was East German, and they met here in London at a Joe Loss jazz concert at the Hammersmith Palais. My grandma was a newly arrived refugee. She had somehow managed to fall on the wrong side of the Stasi and so had to escape the GDR [German Democratic Republic]. She wasn't in London very long at all before she met my grandfather, and he was pretty much the first person of colour that she'd ever seen! It was about 1958, and my mum was born in 1959. I often think 1950s London, must have been so interesting, with all this large-scale immigration that hadn't really happened before and the live music and everything. My mum says they used to laugh a lot because my grandfather was hilarious.

The thing is, I never knew he was Windrush. Partly because I didn't hear about it, I didn't really know about Windrush, and definitely not the Indian-Caribbean Windrush. I knew my grandfather was Indian, and from the Caribbean, but I didn't fully understand. I never really knew about either side of my heritage because in school you don't really learn about East Germany. And grandma didn't really want to talk about it because of everything she went through. It was the same on my granddad's side – I would say. 'Oh, we're from India, but also from the Caribbean.' I just vaguely knew that background. I didn't learn anything about indenture in school either.

I was at a job interview once, and I was saying, about my grandfather, 'He was from the Caribbean and he saw these adverts saying come and help rebuild the country,' and they said, 'Oh, so he was Windrush?' And I was like, 'No, he was Indian' – so I really didn't think we were part of Windrush because I never knew him, and I also didn't really know about the Indian-Caribbean Windrush.

When I was a teenager, I wasn't that interested in my heritage. I just wanted to hang out with my friends and I'm white, so I've never felt that I didn't fit in. Maybe if I had, then that would have driven me to find my heritage a bit more. But now I feel some cultural differences in the way I've been brought up. My mum is half-German, half Indian-Caribbean, and *there are* a lot of differences between her way and the English way – so I feel different now, culturally, than I used to.

Do you know why your grandfather came to the UK?

You know you were saying, although indenture was exploitative, some people did okay? My great-grandfather was quite rich, so he came over, my grandfather, came over with a bit of money which he wanted to invest in a construction firm. But then he was under all this pressure to get a white-collar job, so he didn't do that. But he also wanted to be an actor! I think he's actually an extra in *Bridge Over the River Kwai*! So, in some ways, he made his dream come true. That's the other thing, because all these other people came over for very different reasons, but no, he wanted to be an actor! He wanted to marry a blonde and become an actor – and he did marry a blonde, and he kind of became an actor! But he didn't make money doing that, so he did work on the Underground. In terms of the job, it was a decent job, he worked in the ticket office, and he actually rose quite high and became manager of a tube station, but I can't remember which one. But he did night shifts, and that made him have insomnia, and that really affected him. My mum has always said that there should be something in the London Transport Museum about the Windrush [generation] because they made such a contribution.

I think that he felt very British, as far as I understand – when he came over – he felt very British – and he loved cricket. What's probably quite similar to most people's stories is that they [Windrushers] weren't really welcomed at all. He thought that he was going to be welcomed. The other thing was they were quite well off in Trinidad, so he didn't think of himself as poor at all. He was beaten up a lot here in racist attacks. My mum says that he would come back with broken teeth, because he rode his bike everywhere he'd get dragged off his bike, and then he'd say to mum, 'Oh, we can't judge them, they don't know what they're doing, they're just stupid.' It was in the days of 'No Blacks, No Dogs, No Irish'.[1] That made it difficult for them to find somewhere to live at first. Mum told me she remembers my grandma calling up hotels and being like, 'He's not Black, but he's very dark.' Because he was very, very dark-skinned, almost black. I think their story together is such a London story. Where else would an East German meet an Indian-Caribbean? My mum often says I wouldn't exist if it wasn't for London, and believe that.

Being the child of a Spanish woman who came here around the same time as your grandmother, I know that my mum experienced a lot of abuse for crossing the colour-bar. Was that your grandmother's experience?

---

1   Charlotte is referring to the infamous hand-drawn signs placed in the windows of hotels and rooms available for rent that were intended to actively discriminate against Black, Asian and Irish communities in the 1950s and 1960s. These signs prevented many from finding accommodation.

I know that my grandma didn't have many friends, but a lot of that was to do with the Stasi, she just didn't trust people, you know? She was also very career-driven, she became a headmistress and then an OFSTED [Office for Standards in Education, Children's Services and Skills] inspector. She was very independent. I know more about the racism my grandfather experienced than how their relationship affected how she was treated. But then, being German, that was difficult as well, after the war. She was spat at on the street, but that, as far as I understand, was because she was German, rather than because she married an Indian-Caribbean man. But who knows?

In some ways, they did integrate. They had a life here, and they had decent jobs, but they never stepped outside that life. My grandmother had this one Russian friend, and we really don't know how she had this one Russian friend, but she would joke and say, 'I met her in the British museum when she was carrying an umbrella' – like in a spy story! My grandfather loved going to jazz clubs and he had some friends there, but it still wasn't easy. There was a lot of racism. I definitely feel that he had that enjoyment of life. I mean, is that a Caribbean thing or is that just a cliché? But when he came here, it seemed to him that everyone was just miserable, and he just loved life – he was just cheerful and loved life. That's my mum's personality too.

When my mum was growing up in Putney, she did have some racism against her. She had these two competing identities in terms of her upbringing, but she was also born and growing up in Britain. When she was little, she said, 'I'm Anglo-Indi-Germ-dad!' When she was older, it was like, 'I'll just be a Londoner.' There's that idea in London, which I hope survives, that everyone can be a Londoner. I definitely didn't have much Indian-Caribbean influence growing up at all. My mum and I would, like, to go to Trinidad together, and we'd like to go to Saalfeld together, which was my grandmother's village in East Germany. When she had dementia, in the care home, my grandmother would ask,

'Are we going home now? Back to Saalfeld?' And that was one of the last things she said to me. But she hadn't lived there for so many years, she left when she was 26. I found it sad, because I thought after all these years maybe that was still her home in her heart.

In the first conversation we had, the impression I got from you, when you were talking about your life and your brothers' lives, is that you would all wish to be seen as part of this migration?

Yes, I think we have it dismissed so much, because we're white, like it's not part of me at all; but it's had a huge influence on me [the Windrush story]. I think that mixed-heritage is the right way to talk about, because it is *your* heritage and it does take the issue of skin colour out of it. Brexit is one of the reasons I became more interested in Indian-Caribbean history. Brexit wasn't about just Europe, the underlying nationalism of it made people feel … for example, I've always just thought of myself as a Londoner, but for the first time after the Brexit vote, I thought maybe even I'm not British in the way people want me to be British. It wasn't just about European citizens, it was this nationalist wave that was quite unsettling. It makes sense because of my German side that I would feel the severing of an identity, but it wasn't just that, it was also my Indian-Caribbean side.

I wanted to ask one last thing, what would you like people to know about this migration story as far as it concerns you?

The exploitation and the racism [...]. It's really important to know the story of exploitation in terms of indenture. But when you see photos of them on the boat – and they're all so smart in their suits, and they were such a diverse group of people, even though they were pigeon-holed later. They were invited and then unwelcomed.

My granddad was British, but he was also Indian, and Caribbean, and he was his own person as well. It's important to tell the story of indenture and of what happened here [the racism the Windrushers experienced in the UK], but also that they were people with their own stories and aspirations.

Contributor Biographies

Charlotte Bailey is a journalist based in London. After achieving a BA in Social Anthropology and an MSc in International Development Management from the London School of Economics, she worked in media and peacebuilding in Brussels, Beirut and London. She now writes on human rights, justice and culture for outlets including *TIME*, *The Atlantic*, *The Guardian* and BBC Radio 4. Her grandfather arrived in London from Trinidad in the 1950s and was part of the Indian-Caribbean Windrush generation.

David Dabydeen worked at the University of Warwick's Yesu Persaud Centre for Caribbean Studies for over two decades. He is an award-winning poet and novelist, and has taken part in a number of programmes on British radio and television. He has served as Guyana's Ambassador to China and Guyana's Ambassador and Permanent Delegate to the United Nations Educational, Scientific and Cultural Organization. Professor Dabydeen is now the Director of the Ameena Gafoor Institute for the Study of Indentureship and Its Legacies.

Mr Gee is a spoken word poet whose work has featured in *The Times*, *The Guardian* and *The New Statesman*. He has presented several poetry shows for BBC Radio 4 and National Prison Radio. He was a host for the 2018 Commonwealth Heads of Government Forum in London and is an advisor for the prisoner rehabilitation charity Switchback. In 2020, he created a poetical digital art piece called 'Bring Me My Firetruck' which was showcased at Tate Britain for its *Blake Now* series.

Tao Leigh Goffe is an Assistant Professor of Literary Theory and Cultural History at Cornell University in New York. A writer and a DJ, she specialises in the narratives that emerge from histories of race, debt and technology. Her writing has been featured in *Small Axe*, *The Boston Review* and *Women and Performance*. She received her BA in English from Princeton University and her PhD in American Studies from Yale University. Professor Goffe is the founder of the Dark Laboratory and Afro-Asia Group.

Maria del Pilar Kaladeen is an Associate Fellow at the Institute of Commonwealth Studies in London, working on the system of indenture in Guyana and its representation in literature. She is the co-editor of *We Mark Your Memory* (London: Institute of Commonwealth Studies, 2018), the first international anthology on the system of indenture in the British Empire. Her life-writing has been published in *Wasafiri* and the anthology *Mother Country: Real Stories of the Windrush Children* (London: Headline, 2018), which was longlisted for the Jhalak Prize in 2019.

Lainy Malkani is a London-born journalist and writer with Indian-Guyanese roots. Her critically acclaimed two-part series for BBC Radio 4 *Sugar, Saris and Green Bananas* inspired the creation of a contemporary collection of short stories about the migration of indentured Indians, *Sugar, Sugar: Bitter-sweet Tales of Indian Migrant Workers* (London: HopeRoad Publishing, 2017). She is currently a Senior Lecturer in Media Communications at the University of Arts London.

Nalini Mohabir is an Assistant Professor of Postcolonial Geography at Concordia University in Montreal. Her work focuses on the Caribbean diaspora and indentureship. She is the co-editor of the edited volume *The Fire That Time: Transnational Black Radicalism and the Sir George Williams Occupation* (Montreal, Canada: Black Rose Books, 2021), which recovers the transnational connections of Canada's largest anti-racism student protest in 1969. Professor Mohabir's writing has also been published in *Small Axe*, *The Caribbean Review of Gender Studies* and *Asian Visual Diasporic Cultures and the Americas.*

Elly Niland was born in Guyana and came to the UK in the 1960s. She worked as a teacher in London for many years. An award-winning poet and playwright, she has had two plays commissioned for BBC Radio Four. One of these was a powerful adaptation of Indian-Trinidadian novelist Harold Sonny Laddo's short masterpiece *No Pain Like This Body.* Her short story 'Market Day' was shortlisted for the *Guardian* 4th Estate BAME Prize in 2016.

Jonathan Phang has worked as a television presenter, radio newsreader and TV critic. Although, he is best-known for his role in the hit series *Britain's Next Top Model*, many will remember him for his Caribbean cookery show on Food Network, *Caribbean Cookbook*, and *Gourmet Trains* on the Travel Channel. Jonathan's cookbook *The Pepperpot Club* (London: Hardie Grant, 2013) was nominated for an International Gourmande Award, and is a homage to his incredible culinary heritage and his relationship with the remarkable Guyanese women in his family who formed The Pepperpot Club in his West London childhood home.

Bob Ramdhanie is an arts activist and cultural producer. He co-founded Kokuma Dance Company and a cappella quintet Black Voices, and was the Director of the Black Dance Development Trust. He was commissioned by Arts Council England to research 'Does London Need a Black Dance Centre?' and was awarded an MBE for his contribution to dance. He successfully launched the Rupununi Music & Arts Festival in Guyana and is the Development Director of a National Centre for World Cultures.

Gordon Warnecke was born in Highgate, London and has one son, Daniel. He is an actor, writer and director, and has worked extensively in theatre, performing for the Royal Shakespeare Company and Tara Arts. His television credits include *Only Fools and Horses* and *Holby City*. He was the co-lead in the award-winning film *My Beautiful Laundrette* (1985) and also starred in Franco Zeffirelli's *Young Toscanini* (1988) and the Canadian feature film *Venus* (2017). He has directed three short films. He lives in North London, cooks jerk chicken from scratch, and is a keen Arsenal supporter

Index

The Pluto Press Newsletter

Hello friend of Pluto!

Want to stay on top of the best radical books
we publish?

Then sign up to be the first to hear about our
new books, as well as special events,
podcasts and videos.

You'll also get 50% off your first order with us
when you sign up.

Come and join us!

Go to bit.ly/PlutoNewsletter